T0209325

Overcoming Obstacles

in the

Ed Graves

BALBOA.PRESS

A DIVISION OF HAY HOUSE

Balboa Press books may be ordered through booksellers or by contacting:

Balboa Press
A Division of Hay House
1663 Liberty Drive
Bloomington, IN 47403
www.balboapress.com
1 (877) 407-4847

Print information available on the last page.

ISBN: 978-1-9822-4938-0 (sc)
ISBN: 978-1-9822-4939-7 (e)

Balboa Press rev. date: 06/19/2020

CONTENTS

ACKNOWLEDGEMENTS

Essentially I have found that only thinking people initiate and effect the change in ideas, Challenges and motivations in our lives that last for long periods of time (decades and centuries).

First I would like to graciously acknowledge the first lady in my life Celia Graves, my loving wife of 34 wonderful years. Followed by my three beautiful daughters La'Saundra P. Scott, Tedra N. Graves and Tori S. Graves.

My older brother Willie G.Reaves, Edith Reaves Pearson my older sister who became a heroine in our family when times were tough!

My younger brother and sisters Donald, Wanda and Dorothy Kaye Graves. Dr. Alma Byrd and former Black History teacher Earl Rubin at Morris College. Clarence Scipio who along with my older brother were the first and only ones who believed in me when I approached them with the idea -vision of ON TTRACC BIBLE BUSINESS COLLEGE.

My high school Science teacher Mrs. Anna B. Crawford who first told me that I could do anything in life that I wanted to. My sister in law Clarie McDuffie who has never forgotten me in my times of struggle.

My father and Mother in law who has never shown me anything but sincere and perfect love. My brother in law Stanley Durant, My very good friends Cathy and Xanthine Walker. My lifelong friend and Cousin Arthur Legette, Mrs. Luluwa McDaniel, Diane Edwards and special thanks to mother, Katherine Graves.

INTRODUCTION

Overcoming Obstacles is a vivid account of occurrences throughout my life in a real tough southern existence with a deliberate and mindful dependence on Jesus above all things.

While facing many and sometimes re-occurring trials & test, it was always extremely important that I stayed focused on my dream!

Realizing early on that the spirit of God was within me, and in all things living around me, I found life to be less compelling and much easier to move past fear and hardship.

I grew up in a small community called Rains, in South Carolina and attended all black schools throughout grade-high school and college. I always found it to be relatively easy to develop friendships with both male and female without any trepidation(fear)at all. I welcomed those relationships that I knew would become challenges in the future, I have always been a wholesome competitor at heart.

Many memories flow and continuously surface when I sit down to write after my inspiration comes, I've come to realize that God uses your past to fuel and fertilize your future.

Presently I'm 56 years old, a parent and grandparent as well. I am the founder of ON TTRACC BIBLE BUSINESS COLLEGE which is currently undertaking the development of our own nursing school. This school is designed to teach the fundamental process and philosophy of individuals taking and idea or dream if you will, put it down on paper and assiduously develop it into a course curriculum to follow in order to create a viable business to multiply the wealth for generations to come after us.

Over a century ago great men and women developed businesses-Walter Chrysler, Henry Ford, the Hunts, Heinz, the DuPont's, Mr. Firestone and Charlie Arsenic who developed "poison" along with many others of varying races came to America over time and created an industrial revolution of thriving business which are still generating Billions of dollars for their descendants today. However, those same descendants today are farming those jobs and wealth into other countries where cheaper labor exist with greater profits.

Forty million students graduate from schools and colleges every year who are faced with the task of preparing for an interview for a job which has already been designed for someone else.

The one thing that has been missing in the equation for developing and acquiring the American Dream for black people is Business development and ownership.

A chronicle of events throughout my life which is described in detail to include love, broken trust, justice and injustice, patience, perseverance, strengths and weaknesses. Jesus has without any doubt brought me through the natural vicissitudes of life while I traveled on my journey of pursuing my destiny. The continuous process of patiently although not always so patient, but willing to take the chance or the next step of continuing to learn through trial and error the continuous process of growth which is the key to finding success, never give up!

I would have to say that my married life has been supremely eventful and mostly joyful. My in laws have always been extremely supportive and my sister in law has brought me special joy, even during an outing which we shared some years back during a South Carolina State college homecoming game. I stayed outside tailgating that day while my wife and sister in law went to watch the game, while I did the grill cooking as usual. However that day I couldn't resist the opportunity to make money on food sales because so many people were persistent and desiring to taste my food after the charcoal aroma started navigating the air waves just right. I sold quite a bit of my sister in law's food and kept the profits! my sister in law always made me feel welcome since the first time that I met her and she made me feel loved during holidays.

I had a very special science teacher in high school, Mrs. Crawford who encouraged me to dream, and that I could accomplish anything in life that I wanted to.

Reluctantly, I also have to say and acknowledge that my older sister Edith really blazed a wide trail that I often wished that I didn't have to follow. She was smart and gifted as both a student and teacher who taught me in the tenth grade. That's something that I never liked, imagine having your sister teach you and communicate with all of your other teachers and then go home to talk to your mom every day before you get home.

There was a beautiful young girl in my class whom I thought had real class which I will refer to as L.H. A young woman with recognizable presence so to speak. She had an Indian sounding name and I always admired her but never told her so.

When I was fourteen years of age though in the ninth grade, there was a tall and lankie but good looking girl who moved down to attend our school from Philadelphia briefly. Wouldn't you know that I dated her also to my misfortune, she called me country and ended up teaching me how to smoke cigarettes among other things. Now-that was the dumbest thing that I have ever done. Soon after which I started smoking, about two years later I was drinking and it was sixteen years before I could quit smoking and another fifteen years beyond that before I had to have the help of the Almighty God to quit drinking!

There was a young girl at my church that I had a brief dating experience with, actually two, however one belonged to a girls gang but they were non-violent. Now-I had the good since to know that I was not pulling all of these girls as we used to think, these girls were pulling me! Overall as you will see in this book the many acquaintances that I encountered in my past that has certainly fueled as well as taught me to be aware of the kinds of people that I needed in my life as well as those that I should stay far away from.

At an early age I developed an operative attitude to always look and observe what was going on in a given situation before I spoke or devised an opinion or stance to take. Moreover I remember clearly the things that were told to me by my teachers, coaches parents and all people in authority over me. I was of the opinion that if you studied hard and particularly where sports are concerned, if you practiced diligently with extreme intensity and maintained a listening ear-remain teachable and coachable, develop difficult moves and strategies for both defense and offense, and most of all develop stamina. After perfecting all of the above under normal circumstances success should be eminent; I was also under the impression that an athletic coach's main objective and purpose was to extract-draw out and recognize an athlete's very best potential, talent and gifts." I was very very seriously wrong". At the beginning of my athletic career in the tenth grade at fifteen years old I was the most confident, complete and prepared ball player in many sports and confident as an individual. Gifted in many sports but basketball was the only organized sport that we played at my high school. I spent countless hours watching TV and studying professional NBA players, learning their moves and strategies.

Concerning love! I believe that God allows everyone to fall in love for the experience of getting introduced to love. I don't believe that the first love was ever meant or intended for anyone to hold or keep. Love is the most "powerful" emotion on earth or in heaven, love exist beyond the grave! Falling in love in the early teen years lends itself to the opportunity to become acquainted and gain respect for love itself and to feel it's everlasting pull on the spirit from which it came!!!

CHAPTER ONE

Unique Beginning

As per suggestion of the elevated pontification of thought, considering all avenues present in the mind, and based on God's beginnings, this is a conclusive image of one of a series of advanced conversations that I experienced through my spirit.

Through voluntarily experiencing my own death, I begun to communicate with thought to the two most prestigious Angels that exist in the invisible spirit world! My bedroom is considerably large with beautiful flowers around about.

Multi-colored and multi-fragranced...

Gently and slowly I was drifting in and out from the physical world, into the invisible spirit world. Outside my window was a beautifully manicured lawn with a strategically placed variation of flowers and shrubbery. Back and forth I am able to communicate with the Arc Angel Gabriel, who has power over all truth and repentance and Michael who has been given power over all flesh.

They were conducting Holy questionnaires conclusive of all of my earthly experiences that they had recorded over my lifetime. The questions being asked of me are strategically allowing me to re-visit many adventures that occurred thru out my lifetime. Ideas that I chose to act upon, and those that I decided were simply impossibilities or dreams that I could not bring to pass or completion.

My mind was directed to me being in my mid-nineties, my mind was quiet alert but my body seemed weak and tired. My energy was depleting but I was experiencing no pain. Michael begun by asking me about my activities occurring when I was only four years old, my earliest definitive memory.

My story begins while I was but a small boy living on my Dad's farm in a community called "Rains" in Marion County. Rains is a very small community located approximately seven miles South of Marion on highway 501, and thirty seven miles north of Myrtle Beach. My Dad was the largest black farmer in Marion County, a farm that he inherited when he was only a boy of eleven years of age.

We has six huge pecan trees located on the left side of our house and across the yard a ways. Our yard was quiet large, with three to four acres of beautiful garden in back of the house. "Vegetables "of all kinds and colors to include beautifully red ripened tomatoes, several rows of string beans, some with running vines, "butter beans" yum yum! Okra, squash, water melons, cucumbers and "sugar cane"!

We had plum trees spaced out over the garden, red, purple and some yellow. Some were as large as golf balls. Apple trees were at the end of the rows, and afar off, there were large pear trees with huge beautiful pears, greenish orange in color. An old walnut tree stood at the edge of the woods where I used to play with our dog Brownie. I used to throw walnuts and pine cones for Brownie to retrieve.

I was born Edward Alvanie Graves, however I didn't like the spelling of Alvanie (too easy to mispronounce) so later in life I changed the spelling of Alvanie to Arvanie so that the spelling would accentuate the sound of my name. My date of birth is January 10, 1949 the year representing seven times seven. My Dad had six children from his first wife who's untimely Death was caused by influenza. Respectfully, my mom had four children by her first husband who died unexpectedly also. My Dad had three boys and three girls, as Mom had three boys and one girl, bringing me to become the seventh son of this marriage and first born. Not with standing, my story continues with my earliest definitive memory of an event which occured when I was a toddler, and age that I cannot remember exactly.

It was a cool and brisk fall morning about mid-day, as I was lying on some blankets and under a quilt at the end of some corn rows in one of our fields. I was being both supervised and entertained by one of my older brothers whom we'll call "Billy G". Billy seems to have always been with me for as long as I can remember, all through high school even after school. It was because he cleverly volunteered to ask Mom and Dad to be my baby sitter. I found out later on that Billy wanted to be my caretaker so that he wouldn't have to go to work in the fields along with my other brothers and sisters after school and during the Summer months and harvest time. Billy is ten years older than I am and to continue, Billy asked me if I was cold that morning; of course I said yes and Billy proceeded to gather some sticks, brush and "hay". You see we were at the end of some rows near the walnut tree and six huge haystacks were nearby! It was nippy that day and Billy piled and stacked both wood and hay ---- struck the match and lit the fire.

After starting the fire and we were warming, Billy took a cigarette out of his pocket and lit that too! He was around twelve or thirteen years old so he began to tell me jokes and play around to amuse me to keep me laughing while he puffed his cigarette, cautioning me not to tell. As Billy was mimicking someone shouting funny at Church I was laughing hilariously when a strong fierce wind begun to blow "furiously", whirling dust and leaves around in the air along with the ashes from the fire. Suddenly we noticed that one of the magnificent hay stacks caught fire and burned furiously. And before Billy could do anything to stop it, one by one all six huge hay stacks were burning uncontrollably ! There was absolutely nothing that Billy could do to stop it. I was terrified and so was Billy. Dad was a big man with a deep voice and "huge muscles". Needless to say that I was terrified for Billy, I just knew that he was going to get a rope whipping and get half killed. However, to my surprise as well as Billie's, as soon as Dad came surprisingly when Billy begun to explain the sequence of events leading up to me being cold, and the furious blowing of the wind, Dad just walked away shaking his head, neither Billy or I told Dad that Billy was experimenting with "smoking" that day. Some time passed afterwards and one sunny day while I was waiting at the end of the dirt road with our dog Brownie, Brownie was a great big dog with medium colored brown hair. He was mixed German Sheppard and great Dane. We were waiting for my sisters and brothers to come home from school as we did every day, but this day would prove to be a very special and important day, perhaps the most important day of my life. Normally I would be awakened each morning by the sound of my Dad's deep voice calling my brothers and sisters to wake up and feed the animals before school while mom cooked our aromatic smells of hot biscuits and breakfast!

The sounds of chickens cackling, pigs squealing and cows mooing at day break, easily got me excited every morning. I was usually left at home with Mom and my younger brother who was two years younger than I, he was two and I was four years old. I was saddled with task of looking after my brother while Mom went about her chores of cooking and cleaning the house. Usually around ten or eleven o'clock in the morning when it was warm enough, I was allowed to go outside to play with Brownie without my brother. One day I realized without any doubt, that I had an adversary right outside our door waiting for me, it was our beautiful, golden shinny rooster with a deep red cone laying to the side of his head. I named the rooster "Goldie", I was good at naming animals and toys. Goldie had a "magnificent" huge and shinny tail, he was something special.

Goldie pranced around our yard with his flourishing golden shinny tail like he owned it, and he did when no one was around but me. I would wait until I could look outside the window and see Goldie strutting and prancing with heavy sounding feet, sounding just like a big man. When he went out into the field with the other chickens though, scratching and pecking for food, I would ease outside of the door to find Brownie before Goldie saw me! Most often though he would see me as soon as I stepped out into the yard and "thump, thump, thump", there he was right up in my face and peck me right on my nose. Always before I had a chance to react, Goldie was vicious and deliberate, he was determined to keep me inside the house and there was nothing that I could do but go running inside the house crying to mom.

Goldie's thumping sounding feet sounded like an angry big man running after me as fast as he could. He kept this up for three straight days but then Mom realized that he could put my eye out!

When Friday came that week, just like clockwork my Grandfather came to pick me up as usual to spend the weekend with he and Grandmother. I always had a lot of fun at my Grandfather's house, he would let me do almost anything that I wanted to.

That Monday morning as we were riding back home in my Grandfather's mule drawn wagon he told me something astonishing to say the least, and it has remained with me until this day. "He said that the reason that Goldie, the rooster was chasing me and so intent on challenging and attacking me was because I was born the seventh son in my family". He said that "not only was I special to God, but my Dad would show me favor as well".

LIFE CHANGING MEMORY

My Granddad told me that the reason for Goldie's chasing was because he was determined to be the kingpin of the yard, and after I was born his authority was being challenged by me! Everything would be fine as long as I stayed inside the house, but now that I was venturing into his territory there would be a serious problem with male dominance.

Now that was the most profound and frightening thing that I had ever heard. Furthermore, he said that I couldn't tell anyone because it might bring about envy among my siblings, the same as it did in the Bible story about Joseph in Jacob's family, Joseph was the seventh son by a wife of Jacob to exclude his concubines.

When we arrived in the wagon being pulled by Kate and Mary, Granddad's mules, Kate was a jet black shinny young mule with a powerful looking body, Mary was slightly older but just as fat and well groomed and red in color. Both mules were rapid, high stepping mules and I was fascinated with them both.

When we got home I found it to be somewhat strange and unusual, everything was quiet, too quiet. There was no "Goldie". I stepped down from the wagon very carefully, taking every caution, looking around in all directions before putting my feet on the ground. I was hesitant for sure to see if I could get to the back door before Goldie saw me. I took my last look at Granddad for encouragement or explanation but all I got was a blank stare and somber look from Granddad.

Suddenly! The door burst open and all of my brothers and sisters came running out towards me, "yelling and laughing", they were eager to tell me that my Dad had killed Goldie and he had become part of Sunday's dinner. We always had two kinds of meat on Sundays. I felt both glad and sad for Goldie, he was magnificent, Gold and sparkling shinny when he walked in the sun proudly.

My next thought was of sadness; Goldie was on our table for food. I missed Goldie for a long time after that, and until this day I have never told anyone what my Grandfather told me in the wagon about being the "seventh son".

From that day forward things would be different in my thinking. The way that I saw and perceived things allowed me to except the favor in realizing that the Almighty God had purposefully caused me to be born on the category of the day and number that he hallowed as his day of perfection and completion.

I began to associate as many things as I could think of to the number seven. Although I find no perfection or completion in my life to date and I find it to be quite evasive to say the least.

I found that there were seven letters in the month of my birth, January, and seven letters in my middle name Arvanie, the year of my birth 1949 is seven times "seven"! At our home we always had Bible readings by Mom before bedtime because in those days we didn't have a TV until I was twelve or so.

Ultimately each time that I found myself alone either walking or playing I began to talk to God as if he was right there with me, so much so until I developed a personal relationship with him at a very early age.

Now that we've established what I call a unique beginning, let's continue and cover my most life changing story ! It was the day that I ran down to the end of the road from our house to meet my brothers and sisters coming home from school on the dirt road which is still dirt (unpaved) today. This would become the most definitive day in my life to be sure. One of my sisters brought me and old "Ebony" magazine that was going to be discarded from the school library. I was always interested in the pictures in magazines, Life, Times etc. however this was 1953 and this was the first time I had ever seen a magazine with black people in it! I was excited, on the page of the magazine there was a good looking black man, well dressed indeed. The young man was wearing a beautiful well cut navy blue suit with a soft shine to it. A white shirt with gold cuff links that extended about an inch beyond his suit coat sleeves. He had on a slightly lighter colored blue neck tie with white polka dots. His neck tie reached down exactly even with the bottom of his belt buckle, and his pants were creased to the "Tee".

The young man was standing on a street corner beside a street sign that read "WALL STREET" he was looking up at this tall glass building and carrying a briefcase, although I thought that it was a small suitcase at the time. I ran inside the house and asked Mom what was this sharply dressed young man doing with a suitcase going into this beautiful glass building? Mom took the magazine and looked at it and looked back at me with proud and confident eyes, leaned over looking directly into my eyes and said that this is a briefcase not a suitcase, and that this young man was going into this beautiful building to work in his office! I said his office, yes she said confidently. I said what kind of work he can do with a small brief case, inquisitively? She said that this young man has very important papers inside the briefcase to work from. I was stunned, and then she told me that if I studied hard in school when I was old enough to go that I could become a "very important businessman too"! Wow, my mind was blown.

At that very moment I envisioned that that young man was me and at that moment I knew that I had just discovered my destiny. Never in my life had I ever seen any man black or white, wearing a suit to work, and now I realized that I would be doing that very same thing as the man on the page of the Ebony magazine one day for certain. There it was, my calling, my purpose in life was right there in my hands on the page of an old magazine.

There would be absolutely nothing else in my entire life that I would ever want to do. The young man was going into his own office to work from his own briefcase in a beautiful glass building. Life just doesn't get any better than that in my book. A new door of opportunity had just presented itself to me at the tender age of four. The idea is still as strong today as it was then, to become a successful businessman.

The magazine alone had just opened up a different orientation, a new insight of enlightenment of a new world that I had never known before, I was completely blown away. A black man wearing a beautiful blue suit and tie, going into his own office to work out of his own briefcase, in 1953 "cool".

That night I went to bed with the magazine under my pillow, I would have to find a way to get into school as soon as possible at age five, finish, and do whatever it took to go to work in my own office! Although the original cover page was torn off the first page that was left seemed to be the cover to me.

CHAPTER TWO

Entering My Second Door Of Destiny

During my studies at my Alma Mater, Morris College located in Sumter South Carolina, I was fortunate to get a job in the college bookstore. I fell in love with the philosophy of life introduced and left for us to discover by the greatest ingenious minds on the planet from long ago.

Great men and women like Diocletian, Thales, phericides, Ptolomy, Vertruvious from Egypt, Patanjili from India, permenides, Diogenes, and most of all, "Pathagoras" from Greece; The father of the word Philosophy! I read hundreds of books that were not required readings and all for free. Oh yes I read everything that I could find in our college library as well as the City of Sumter's library about King "Solomon" and the "Queen of Sheba". Through meditation and tenacious concentration, I managed to develop my thinking capabilities well, the one subject that's not taught in the schools in America. Thinking gives me great pleasure and confidence in my future.

I discovered that absolutely anyone can change their very existence on earth simply by thinking and then acting on those thoughts. As I remembered always the young man on the cover of the old raggedy ebony magazine as a child, still opens doors in my mind and allows me to visually see tremendous heights.

The beautiful navy blue suit, three button jacket, a white starched shirt with an inch and a half collar, a polka dot tie that he intentionally caused to hang the tip of the end of his tie exactly parallel to the bottom of his belt buckle. Black Stacy Adams shoes with a black matching briefcase with gold trim corners!

I continued to see that picture throughout my life until I became that man on the cover of the magazine. I have seen in my mind fully constructed for ON TTRACC BIBLE-BUSINESS College many times. Through my dreams I have seen my children and grandchildren inheriting a place to work and expand their minds and hearts along with their bank accounts;

(Belief)

"I believe" that the Mexicans who are constantly in a migratory state, to America, who are part white, part African and part American Indian blood, are simply coming home to re-claim their lands. I'm very glad that God allowed me to be born in a time such that there is no slavery existing openly in America!

"I believe" that the most important thing in life for everyone, regardless of age is to ask God what is their purpose on the earth, and why was I born in times chronically such as these. I enjoy safe sound sleep at night which I do not take lightly, even though gang violence is threatening all of our futures.

"I believe" that once an individual who has truly fallen in love, and then hurt by love for whatever the reason, if you chose to take Wisdom at heart, a wise person will guard and protect their heart more carefully before interring relationships in the future. Being careful about whom you allow to enter your heart will consequently cause you to make better marriage choices.

"Mahatma Ghandi" once wrote that prayer, actually examining your thoughts and guarding your mind, to establish God in your heart is truly wonderful". Prayer is a function of the heart; we speak aloud to wake it up! I have noticed an observed many times in some Pentecostal Churches the open and aloud prayer four and sometimes five times during one morning service. I know that God is everywhere and in all of our hearts and can hear us at a whisper!

"I believe" that our young people are taking a lot for granted by assuming that all things that are available to us now will always be as it is, not true. It is often said that money will not make you happy, perhaps not in a since, well, I have found that to have lived with and without it and to live without money, not only brings about sadness it is sometimes painful! "King Solomon" said that money satisfies all.

"I believe" that as infinite and as deep as the ocean is and as powerful as the Sea is, if one can come to the realization that all of that power is within us, existing in our hearts, there is nothing that we cannot do if we believe it and allow God to help us in his own time and own way.

"I believe" that yesterday's memories are good only if they are good memories, but if we take a look at tomorrow without restraints and attachments and be willing to take the chance that no one else has taken, you will ultimately go far.

I don't believe that one should tell "anyone" all of your ideas and dreams other than God "I believe" that to dream is one of the most important gifts that God has given us. I was and still unto this present day have always been a dreamer, both night and day, both asleep and awake I have always been a dreamer! I have had a schedule of events in my mind to work on in my life, but set no deadlines for completion. I have always been deliberate about most things that I wished to take place in my life and I allow no one to change my mind but God!

By practicing strengthening my faith, the thing that I believe God for I've learned to receive a knowing in my heart without any doubt, as sure as I know the name of the next day, that will come.

If it were my intention to impress someone and it didn't come to pass as I would have liked or didn't work out as I would have liked, it was simply easy enough for me to be impressed with myself, there's no one like "Arvanie" I always said. There nothing prosaic or ordinary about wanting to be the best, it is what I have always wanted and was never afraid to be tested by anyone.

Now, this is a good place to enter my second door of destiny. I turned five years old on January 10, 1954, that was the day that I began to ask my mom and Dad three or four times a day to let me go to school.

I knew that the beginning of September was the starting month for the coming school year. I was extremely bored because the only things that I was allowed to do was to go to the end of the road and look over at the stream that we called the trestle, perhaps throw rocks into and to skid rocks if possible. I had not been given enough time to overcome the obstacle of our rooster Goldie and I did miss him, fear and all;

In the spring of 1954 I took a ride into the township of Rains with Dad where we often stopped on the way home at the Crift's community store. Mrs. Crift, the owners wife was the first grade teacher at our brand new school still under construction and almost complete for the coming school year where I would be among the first students to attend and first to inter in the first grade at the new school. I felt a very compelling urge to take this opportunity to engage and convince Mrs. Crift that not only was I ready and anxious but competent as well.

I had been tutored almost every day after all chores were done and everyone had finished supper. I had convinced both my older brothers and sisters to teach me to spell certain words and to write those words on a straight line. My chance came as soon as I walked into the store.

While dad was talking to Mr. Crift and buying a few essentials, although I later learned that my dad had planned it that way I begun to express to Mrs. Crift just how badly I wanted to go to School. To show her how prepared I was, I began to count and spell words one after the other. Surely enough she was impressed enough to tell dad that I could start school the next fall school year.

Mrs. Crift was a good looking brown skinned lady, short with slightly graying hair. I had no trepidation or fear in my heart; I just stepped right up to her and said Mrs. Crift, my name is Arvanie Graves and I am quite ready to go to school. She came closer to me and leaned over bringing us both face to face and said "Arvanie", I know just who you are, you're Johnnie's boy and you count and spell very well, she then told dad that I could start school the following Fall.

I was very proud of my accomplishment, I had developed an idea and successfully sold myself to Mrs. Crift. At that moment I came to the realization that I had successfully completed the necessary learning process to move away from the rooms of life at home and the farm surroundings and was ready to open the next door of life, one that was unknown to me. The plan concerning the dream of me becoming a Businessman was in place. My first couple of weeks in school went along smoothly, however I soon discovered that there was a "Goliath" in my class, one that was groomed and developed by his older cousins, that I would have to face and defeat.

A wise man once wrote that when a child is born, he enters into a world unknown to it, and there is potentially one thousand rooms with doors to choose from to open and enter. One must keep taking the chance and the next step in life. The mind produces a variety of tremendous thoughts, even when you are asleep the human brain produces dendrites that spring outward, back and forth with thoughts. The problem is that most people continuously think the same thoughts each and every day. Which bill should I pay, what should I have for breakfast, lunch and dinner, how much will gas cost, should I date this guy or girl etc. I've learned to carefully guard my mind and select new thoughts and travel the road less traveled.

I never thought that the problem that I had with our "rooster, Goldie", when pecking me on my nose, was introducing me to some more of the same because I chose not to face my fear of him and devise a plan to overcome that obstacle! Those of us who overcome obstacles are among the most successful and prosperous people on earth.

CHAPTER THREE

Introduction To Wisdom

Goldie was a handsome beautiful and very proud bird! He had become a very important part of my childhood development. "Goldie" was the name that I had given him because one day I stood at my window and saw this big beautiful, yellowish-golden colored rooster walking through the field, prancing and dancing, looking over the other chickens, with the sun shining reflective sparkles from his feathers. He had a beautiful bright red colored robust cone leaning to the side of his head. But nature brings about the natural vicissitudes of life which I refer to as my obstacles. No one ever told me that I could stop Goldie from attacking me, simply by taking a stick and crack him up side his head and then begin to chase him! Notwithstanding, at age four, Goldie was almost as tall as I was and seemed just as big, particularly when he jumped up in my face.

So, at age five I entered the first grade in 1954. Brownie had become my dog now that there was no Goldie, whom I did miss. Brownie followed me to school every day, he and I would always hang back behind my other brothers.

I was always observing things and looking over the fields, capturing all of the new sights, sounds and smells of the forest, wheat and corn fields. I was particularly amused with the way that the wheat leaned over to one side or the other depending on whichever way the wind blew!

The soft gentle breezes blowing and the rays from the sun emanating from the earth during the spring was fascinating! I was always dreaming, I had a big date with my office (in my future) that I just couldn't wait to see. I quickly familiarized myself with the sights and sounds of my new school and the new door of life that I had just opened and entered.

A cousin of mine whom I will call Shelden was living with my Great uncle-and his Grandfather on his farm that we passed by every day on my way to and from school. He was a year older than I was and had started school a year earlier but got left back and would now be in my class. Every day Sheldon had attracted a crowd at the entrance of the school as he asked me to box every day, and every day we boxed to a draw. We were equally matched and put on a good boxing exhibition for the huge crowed that we entertained each morning. I had been well trained in the art of pugilism (boxing) by my older brothers before I entered school. In those days if you didn't know how to fight, you might as well stay at home if you didn't want to get beaten up every day by anyone who chose to beat up on you anytime that they felt like it!

My cousin Sheldon and I were the class champions, I was naturally gifted. I was good. As the years went by and we entered the third grade we had both become famous for not only our boxing skills but other sports as well.

One cold morning my cousin didn't come to school for some reason and there was a boy in my class who seemed to always hang around us while we were at lunch, or playing or whatever. This boy was a real light skinned kid about the exact same size as I was, Sheldon was a tad larger. This boy was seven then, the same as I was but he always seemed timid and shy. As I walked onto the campus this cold morning, would you believe that this kid had gathered a huge crowd, a gathering that had been fostered or instigated by his much larger cousins in higher grades, and were whooping it up about a boxing match between myself and the little light skinned scary kid in my class. It seemed that this kid had felt that he had been in the background long enough and he wanted his share of the fame. He had watched and saw how I was able to throw punches from either side with both hands, uppercuts and right hand crosses, combinations and such. His cousins had taught him how to throw a right hand lead punch and hit the nose to win the match by default or TKO if you can't continue. The key trick to this plan was to throw the right hand lead before I was ever ready or into a boxing stance with my fist up for protection. It was a dirty trick and I fell for it.

This boy was a frightened timid boy so I was very surprised when they asked me to box with him. My cousin and I had previously boxed every morning but this day he was out of school and the opening was available for this boy to become famous, however I thought that this was a big tease that I would accommodate and provide some friendly entertainment for the huge crowd that had been waiting for me (a champion) to show up.

I couldn't believe it! As soon as I put my books down, didn't get a chance to even warm my hands, and before I could put my fist up, "wham" he threw the right hand lead punch and hit me right on the bridge of my nose. The pain was debilitating, my eyes weld up with water and I began to cry. for the pass two and a half years I had boxed and put on a fascinating boxing exhibition, boxing with my cousin Shelden to a draw or one day I was declared the winner and the next day he was the winner, never any tricks we were both honorable competitors and remained friends who played together, now things would be different. Not only was I hurt I was embarrassed and surprised.

This little light skinned scary boy who had been hanging around Shelden and I every day for protection, and to be included in the company of the two most famous boys in the entire school, not only had he just beaten me without me ever having thrown a punch, he had instantly developed fame and the title of the "BROWN BOMER", the title that was given to our hero and heavy weight champion of the world, Joe Lewis. All during classes that day there was whispering and laughing, no one was talking to me or asking me what had happened to me, everyone was gathered around the newly crowned champion, the Brown Bomber!

At lunch time I found out what all of the giggling and whispering was about. This boy had gotten with his cousins again and was prepared to do the same thing all over again, this boy loved the attention that he was getting and had been missing all before while he stayed in the background. He was prancing around like a rooster! Needless to say, I didn't even get to eat my lunch that day before this boy had sneaked me with the exact same punch before I could even get my hands up. It was a sad walk home that day just Brownie and I.

I couldn't wait, my brothers Billy and PJ Had spent a lot of time training me and teaching me the skills of boxing before I ever went to school. How to always keep my eye on my opponent and watch both his hands and eyes, the eyes would always tell you when your opponent was anticipating his next punch to throw. I had been taught well and I found out that familiarity with anything gave you confidence. Trust me I was indeed confident, any sport that I liked, I had the God given talent to execute and execute with ease.

A GOLIATH IN MY CLASS

When I got home that day I immediately went to the mirror to see if my nose looked any different. Even though the punches were very painful, there was no blood or swelling thankfully.

I couldn't wait for my big brothers PJ and Billy to get home from the local high school. My brother Billy and I seemed to always have had a special connection to each other so I approached him first with my dilemma. As soon as I told the story in detail to Billy he immediately realized that I had been sat up–and he told me quiet emphatically that what else was wrong with the picture that I was painting for him was that I simply quit too soon. He said that it was an old trick used to steal my thunder and become famous at the same time.

He said that after the Brown Bomber had hit me with his best shot and I was still standing and there was no blood, even though I was in pain there was absolutely nothing else to lose, nothing else that he could do to me and it was the time then to show the world what I was made of and to let go with both hands and he knew there was no one who could stand up to me when I began to throw flurries and combinations like I had been taught.

My brother PJ told me something that I will never forget, "powerful". He said that it is very important when boxing or fighting to always keep your eye on anyone who could be a potential threat, and when getting into a boxing stance, just before you throw a punch, you should always tighten your fist as tight as you can so that when your hands make contact, not only will you deliver greater pain to your opponent, it prevents you from hurting your hands.

I sparred and faked in shadow boxing all afternoon while I imagined that I had the little Goliath in front of me. PJ placed his hands up open on both sides of his head as I practiced my speed and accuracy until bedtime. All that I could think of was that when I left school that day I saw the little light skinned boy being held up on the shoulders of his cousins and the crowd cheering the phrase "THE BROWN BOMBER", To the little scary boy who had fame for a day.

On the way to school the next day my brother Billy played hooky from school, he was as anxious as I was, he knew that I was ready and a wholesome competitor. I loved competition, I knew that I was gifted, I loved boxing and I loved to fight!

All the way on the walk to school the next morning I was anxious and excited in the anticipation of my calculated demise of the little light skinned scary boy who had taken my title and fame through trickery and planning by his cousins. I couldn't get it out of my mind the things that Billy and PJ had told me. It would become the wisest thing that anyone had ever told me. If you are in battle and you are already hurt and surprised, it is the time then to let go and strike with all of your might and power, your know how with both hands and let your opponent feel your power! There's nothing else to lose only things to gain.

As soon as I came in view of the campus and stepped on the school grounds, all that I heard was the chanting and excitement that this little boy had gained. It was nostalgia for fame in the air as if we were boxing for money! This is the very reason that no boxing champion in any weight class can retire a champion, he has to be beaten and the title taken from him just like I was about to do this tricky kid.

My cousin never believed that this boy had defeated me anyway, he knew that the reason that he and I were the most popular boys in the entire school and we were only in the third grade, was because we had extreme courage and we were good.

When I went to put my books down I never took my eyes off of my Goliath, I turned sideways and just let the books fall. Brown Bomber had been exercising his bragging rights and had suddenly gained nerve and confidence. IT didn't matter though, Billy had already started to laugh when I made my approach while this boy was giggling. The plan was that he would wage his attack while I was still cold from my walk to school, he rode the bus. Everyone was expecting to see the same thing happen all over again, but before the kid knew it I was the one on the attack. As soon as my books hit the ground I rushed right up with hands blazing, I threw the left jab like text book quickly followed by the right cross with combinations and hooks to the left and then to the right and back up to the head with fury! I had my right hand cocked to throw the finishing blow when his cousin stepped in and covered him protecting him from me and anymore damage and pain that I inflicted on him.

This little light skinned boy was hollering as if I was killing him. He was glad to be taken out of my reach. Knots rose up over both eyes and his entire face was "red", knots on his head, sides bruised you name it, everywhere I hit him was red.

Now—all of this hype might seem barbaric, however in all sincerity, we were both too small and only seven years old, too small to hurt each other anymore than lumps and bruises. Throughout my entire grammar, grade school and high school did I ever see anyone get much more than that. Never saw anyone suffer anything more, this kid had been skillfully taught to throw a right hand lead to the nose but if there was any mistakes in both timing and the placement of the blow, then this kid was in trouble because he didn't have anything else to fall back on and no courage. Everything depended upon his opponent being disabled immediately after the punch landed, after that gamble he had no other recourse. That morning I had absolutely no fear, this boy was all mine. Afterwards two thoughts came to my mind, the word Goliath disappeared from my memory along with the words "Brown Bomber".

From that day forward I wasn't able to get anyone to box with me. My fame grew and I continued to practice. I went up to higher grades to try and get someone to box with, but there was no one willing to accommodate me. I became the sole boxing champion in my school and no one ever called that young man Brown Bomber ever again and I will only refer to him as BB here after.

After defeating my Goliath completely I went inside the school building to the bathroom to be alone, to do some quiet thinking.

"Humm", sixty thousand thoughts per day huh, thoughts that spring out in all directions called Dendrites springing back and forth from the brain, measured by neurologists, Doctors who study the mind and capabilities of the brain as seen under a powerful microscope, appearing as seven times smaller than a period at the end of a sentence.......

All that it took for me to be moved from the top of the chart of popularity in the eyes of the crowds of our schoolyard, was to simply be tricked' hood winked by and envious little light skinned boy. This boy would have to live in my shadow again now but this time it would be in the form of humility and infamy; After everyone saw how I overcame that obstacle, everyone wanted to beat up on BB, and I do mean everyone; He was subjected to all kinds of ridicule and open challenges. BB had to hide behind me for protection everyday all threw grade school, high and college. We developed a lifelong friendship that I knew was always based on a lie...

CHAPTER FOUR

Opening New Doors

A t the age of seven I was only in the third grade when I was appointed as the Sunday school teacher at my local Church. We'll call it "Hope Church" because I thought it really could use some help in the thinking department and sadly that's my sincere feelings about that Church today.

At Hope Church we seemed to quiet frequently have professional singing groups to appear at our Church for various functions and fundraisers and Church outreach endeavors. This was the catalyst for the discovery of many professional singing groups to spring up out of our Church. So, before the programs begun, sometimes I would be asked to do short speeches.

One Sunday morning as I was conducting Sunday school class which was comprised of not only the youths but some adults as well, These adults were individuals who had not yet confessed that they had received the "Holy Ghost "yet. As we began to read in unison the passage of scripture that reads "Lo, I will be with you always, even to the ends of the earth".

Arvanie, I will be with you always, even to the ends of the earth! There was no mistake in my judgment, I had heard the still small voice many times. I knew at that moment that I had heard the voice of the "Holy Spirit".

As the days went by following the revelation I began to talk with Jesus when I was alone, so much so that I developed a personal friendship type relationship with him. My uncle was the Superintendant of our Church and Sunday school-he was a wise man indeed. At home my Mom frequently read Bible stories at night to get us familiar with the scriptures. Mom had received the Holy Spirit at the age of eight and she didn't take the teachings of the Bible lightly.

It would be that coming summer in summer Bible school that I was asked to select a Bible character and story to do a Bible report in Church that following Sunday. My choice of character was the tenth son of King David "KING SOLOMON". While reading and researching the scriptures I discovered that the young fifteen year old King Solomon, newly crowned King chose a quiet solome night to go out into the desert, after careful thought, he prayed and asked God to grant him the Wisdom to be able to rule fairly over the great number of people above all things; The young King had been raised in the palace of his rich father, the great King David who was not only rich, Solomon witnessed Frequently lift up the name of the Lord in Prayer. Solomon was already wise to a degree at the age of fifteen when he took his oath as King so he used that wisdom to ask God for wisdom to rule over the diverse colony of people with the different cultures and ethnicities that he was responsible for.

God answered his unselfish prayer and blessed him with an abundance above and beyond any request by any King ever before and after him. He would become the richest and wisest King that has ever lived. So, it didn't seem too over the top for me to begin asking for the same thing, I was highly impressed with the thinking of King Solomon! I began to dream and imagine myself to be a King and would later find substantiating Bible scripture to support my claim to be a "KING". I began my search for wisdom which continues until this day.

QUEST FOR WISDOM

When I was in College years later I discovered that the reason that King Solomon chose wisdom above wealth an all things was when he displayed that wisdom by discerning between the two prostitutes who had the infamous dispute over a living child (infant) who was to be decided upon by a woman's intrinsic intuition.

A husband and wife, for example, can go out for an evening of relaxation and pleasure and find themselves miles away from home while their young child is left with a baby sitter. The child suddenly begins to experience trauma through an accidental mishap and is suffering some type of pain or danger, the mother will intrinsically know that something's wrong instinctively, with her child and tell her husband to go back to where the child is to check on him or her, while the husband has absolutely no clue as to what or how the wife knows and he doesn't! (it happened to me).

I also discovered that "Bath Sheba" King Solomon's mother was from Ethiopia Africa, the new name for CAANAN. which was the name of "Black Ham", the oldest son of "NOAH". It was Bath Sheba who sent for the Queen of Sheba.

Now back to the episodes of the third grade which are many, I was also in my first acting play, and educationally I maintained in the top two or three in my class. Academically I had an exceptional memory. When I was selected and given my part in the play to learn, it just seemed easier to learn the entire play to get a feel for my character and others and the times and settings for where the incidents took place. By learning everyone's part it seemed easier for me to no my cue to speak.

I was given the part of the black King in the play "we three Kings". BB, the little light skinned boy and my cousin Sheldon played the other two Kings, the three of us hung together you see but it was different after BB used the trickery in boxing the day Sheldon was out of school. Everyone in and out of school knew that BB had only pretended to be my friend while watching every day for three years from the first grade through the third, figuring out a way to beat me and become famous at my expense. BB couldn't even ride the bus to school without me standing beside him or him behind me for his protection because everyone wanted to beat him up for being so dirty towards me and they also found out just how scary and cowardice and unskilled as a boxer he was. After I took him apart that day that I took my revenge and retaliation upon him he was pitiful, he would walk a couple of miles each morning to my house so that he could walk to school under my protection, I kept everyone off of him.

That night when I finished my chores and having dinner, I went directly to my room that I shared with my two brothers an begun to read and reread the play. I became so evolved in my part as the black King, I learned the entire play in just a few hours. The next morning I was excited, I thought that I would impress my teacher when I got to school with my learning capabilities when we practiced the play. Well, everyone in my class was shocked, except my teacher that is. No one else even knew one line of their part in the play and here is this black kid Arvanie Graves, the dark one in the bunch who knew not only all lines of his part in the play, he knew the entire play and was telling the others what and when it was time to speak. Not only was my teacher not impressed with my accomplishments with learning, she was angry at me for making the others students look bad.

Perhaps this is a good time to describe the mentality of black people in the 1950's pertaining to skin color. You see—lighter skinned people were presumed to be smarter than darker skinned people and perceived to look better in general appearance. The darker you were the uglier you were and easier to dismiss you and any accomplishments that you made, you never got any credit for anything good, only blamed for everything bad that happened;

Lighter skinned people on the other hand were expected to be smarter and more gifted in everything, I mean everything. Gifted in things not only pertaining to the mind but physical attributes as well. The lighter your skin color was the more gifted in everything you were expected to be,--in everything.

I was extremely shocked and deeply hurt by my teacher, she was a beautiful red woman, short, about five foot five with dark black wavy hair. All three of us had a crush on her and others as well. In the fourth grade I had a real dark skinned female teacher who treated me the exact same way, discriminated against by the dark and the light skinned teachers and haven't even met or encountered a real white person yet. My third grade teacher scolded me for during good and just made me wait to participate in the play until the others caught on by learning their parts, weeks!

My teacher simply over looked the idea that I had learned every line of the entire play in one night and no one else had even taken the initiative to learn the title of the play. Now just imagine my state of mind at this point, I looked around the classroom at every dark skinned kid in my class and saw the effect of the rejection that they all felt for me. It had become an order of acceptance to realize that if you were black, you could and very often would be rejected for even during good.

The night of the play we all did well, my cousin Sheldon and BB were the three kings and we all remained friends until this day. That night on stage however, I seemed to have had an optical illusion as one by one we three kings handed our gifts to the young girl who played the part of Mary the Mother of Jesus. unfortunately the doll that was used as the newborn baby Jesus was a white doll! We were in a candle lit tent with the lights dimmed both on stage and in the audience which seemed to me the white doll was so very badly out of place. Everyone on stage and in the audience were dark complexioned and the Jesus doll was white, in the Holy land where everyone is of color. I knew in my heart instinctively that Jesus was not white! It just didn't feel right. Later research would reveal Just that, Jesus was not white. On the way home in Dad's car that night I told both mom and dad two very significant revelations that I had just encountered; One, that Jesus could not have been white as everyone thought, and secondly, that I was going to marry Lynn, the little girl who played the part of Mary the Mother of Jesus. Dad laughed hilariously and told me that I would have to get a job right away.

I was beginning to realize that my life was being molded and shaped by those directly around me and functioning in my inner circle of life; Every morning while walking to school, Brownie, our dog had now become my dog, We spent so much time playing and frolicking together that he begun to follow me to school each day. He waited out in the edge of the woods at school every day until the last school bell rang and I ran to the edge of the campus to meet him.

The third grade was very eventful and taught me that there were some very significant black people in our history that had been intentionally left out of our academic studies however I was an avid Bible reader and I found that there were some great black people recorded in the books of Genesis through Malachi, that I was able to verify later in my college research.

There is a book called (The Black Presence in the Bible) written by Rev. Dr. Walter A. McCray takes us back to the "Antediluvian" era (the period before the flood) some very important facts exists concerning probably the oldest city in the world. The "Hittites were one of the most powerful warrior African tribes and the first to use the alphabet, also referencing "Uriah the Hittite"!

Uriah, Bath Sheba's husband, Whom King David ordered to be killed in battle was a Hittite! After the flood, Noah's three sons represent three nationalities of people—Shem was of the Oriental nation, Japheth was of the white Nation. "Ham" the black African had four sons. CAANAN, which today is the old name for Ethiopia! EGYPT, CUSH and PHUT, the old name for Somalia![1]

The sons of Cush were Seba, Havila, Sabta, Raamah and Sabteca. The sons of Raamah, Sheba and Dedan. Cush was also the father of "Nimrod" the great hunter! Egypt became the father of the Philistines, which makes the infamous "GOLIATH" the giant a derivative of the black race. During further studies I became aware of the fact that not only were black people discriminated against by white people but black people as well. Many black students dropped out of school before ever reaching the sixth grade for that very reason. The day that I looked into the eyes of the dark complexioned students after my teacher treated me as if I had committed a serious crime by memorizing the school play, We Three Kings, I saw rejection and hopelessness in their faces.

It has always been clearly understood by me and some others that black people are for the most part, some skillful and powerful people. I guess the white kids resolved to the idea that we were too dumb to realize that we had actually beaten them in almost everything that we chose to. I knew that black people in the bible and In my community were the real deal and there was absolutely no way to change my thinking.

---

[1] "Now these are the generations of the sons of Noah, Shem, Ham, and Japheth: and unto them were sons born after the flood." Genesis 10:1 KJV

The most powerful and most intelligent people in my opinion were indeed very black. So, when anyone called me nigger, I simply resorted to what I had learned in Bible school. As soon as anyone called me the N-word it gave me great and refreshing pleasure to simply take the power from the word by expressing the fact that the wisest man who ever lived was King Solomon, who has a black mother (Bath Sheba-from Ethiopia) and further more he is in our Holy BIBLE!

I also strengthen my position by dropping names like the great Wilt Chamberlain! Bill Russell, Joe Lewis the former heavy weight champion of the world in the 1940's when all odds were against him. I would say that these men and many others are niggers and I'm certainly proud to be among the race that produced these men and women that I frequently named such as Althea Gibson, Wilma Rudolph and let's not forget Mahailia Jackson, now--, who do you know that's comparable to these folks. And furthermore, what would you suggest that we do competitively that you can beat me doing! That's just what I thought, silence.

ABOUT THE N-WORD-NIGGER

At a very early age I discovered before ever moving up from the third grade that being called Nigger by white people had very little negative effect on me. In the community that I grew up in after our house burned down at our farm I saw and became very familiar with relatives of mine who were some great men of valor indeed.

There was a cotton gin almost in the center of Rains with a depot where the train stopped to pick up passengers on its way to towns like Marion, Mullins, and further North. Farmers came and sold their produce as we did also. We sold cucumbers and tomatoes etc.

My older brother and I would often go to the cotton gin to watch the machines extracting the seeds from the cotton but more importantly, we went to see the big and "powerful" black men at work. Some worked with their shirts off and some worked with their shirt sleeves cut off a short ways down from their shoulders so that you could see bulging, powerful "muscles" protruding out. The men liked the idea that we were so fascinated with the great strength and raw power that they displayed. There a was tall and huge in statue man named Eddie, and two other brothers who were my cousins and equally as big and as strong as Eddie was. These men ranged in height from six foot five inches to six foot seven. We'll call my cousins Turk and Terry! These three men could easily pick up thirteen or fourteen hundred pound bales of cotton! No joke! Every day they would take turns picking up a bale of cotton and walk with it.

There were also some cousins of mine who could pick up the rear end of a Packard car, that's heavy. I saw these things with my own eyes so there is no tall tales involved in this matter.

One day I took a ride down in Mullins with dad and while I was sitting in the car waiting for dad to get finished talking with a man who rubbed my dad the wrong way and right out of the blue dad hit with a punch that sent the guy rolling under our car. Each time the man got up dad hit and put him down again as if he didn't believe it, until the third knockdown he wasn't able to get up.

There was a white family whom we used to help gather their tobacco during the summer, the days that we weren't gathering our own or my uncle's. The two white boys were about the same ages as my brother and the other was my age. We played with those boys every day, we competed in swimming, wrestling and foot races. Now certainly you do realize that in those days when you beat the white boys during anything, they immediately called you "Nigger" and not only that, they always seemed to figure out a way to invalidate the contest. The word Nigger seemed to always be the one word that whites used to belittle you or your accomplishment and made them feel as if they didn't really loose to a real person, Nigger doesn't count. It bothered my brother but to me it simply seemed that there was something missing from their thinking.

CHAPTER FIVE

Beginning My Basketball Career

My principal, Mr. Noben from elementary school was my first encounter with a male influence and was to be a very positive one from the very beginning, and one that lasted until his death years later.

Mr. Noben was a very fair man in his relationships and treatment of his students. A man with dark black curly hair and a light colored skin complexion. He was about five foot eight inches tall and left handed. He was the first adult male teacher who did not show favoritism toward anyone because of their skin color. He also had a great love and respect for an individual's study habits, athletic and intellectual abilities as well. Mr. Noben showed me favor because I was blessed to be graced with both intellectual and athletic abilities of a high degree.

However he favored a couple of other students who were gifted in both those areas as well so I wasn't singled out, which I was comfortable with. I was gifted in the sport of baseball, football, basketball and I was the school's boxing champion in the six grade. In those days there was no middle school, you graduated from the six and moved onto another school which was the high school beginning with the seventh grade.

I was told that I had excellent hand to eye coordination and quickness which allowed me to play and excel in any sport that I chose to play that were available and had access to. Mr. Noben was excited about my abilities and would often reward me with small gifts like candy bars or a free lunch. I liked the free lunches so in the fifth grade I asked Mr. Noben for a job moping the bathroom which provided the lunch for me and younger brother.

Mr. Noben was promoted to become the principal at my high school the same year that I went there which made my transition move smoothly. My name was called a lot in conversation and over the PA system when he wanted to talk to me and give me good advice.

At this juncture I will call my high school (LB) high to protect the identity of some of the characters that I will mention in this chapter.

LB high school was a newly constructed school in 1954, the same year that my elementary school was built. The school was a single A, meaning that there was around one thousand students attending the school, all black and hailing from varying distant communities in what was District three. The school remained all black, as did all public schools in South Carolina until nineteen sixty eight.

My very first day at LB I was awe struck when I entered the enormously huge and magnificently breath taking gym! It was beautiful. The ceiling was extremely high and the floors were beautifully polished and shinny. The bleachers were polished and shinny also. No one was allowed to even walk across the corners of the floor with hard bottom shoes on.

The basketball coach at LB high was a lean slender built man about five foot nine inches tall with a voice of spontaneity to complement his neat appearance. The coach had a winning reputation that was unmatched by any other coaches in the district and was revered by everyone. His reputation was impeccable; We'll call him coach Lefton! We had both football baseball and basketball teams my first couple of years at LB high but that was soon to change, coach Lefton had the kind of power of persuasion such that He encouraged our Principal and school board to eliminate our football and baseball teams permanently, In order for him to have access to all athletes for his basketball team to win championships in the years to come. When both the football and baseball teams were eliminated it afforded coach the opportunity to use those players to practice basketball all year long none stop! Coach Lefton was the most famous coach in the territory. In my opinion, his fame was due to the fact that in most cases when other schools were practicing baseball in its season and football in its season, we were practicing the almighty basketball as it were, relentlessly all year long, he stayed ahead of the game. Coach Lefton's efforts were centered solely on the one sport that he optioned, "basketball".

HEROISM VS COURAGE

My lifelong friend Lee, who is also my cousin, lived across the railroad tracks behind our house in Rains. Anyone will tell you even to this day that when you saw one of us you also saw the other. Lee and I were entrepreneurs even in those early days, if there was any way for a kid to make some honest money, we could find it. We competed in everything and certainly that would place sports at the top of the list.

There was a small lake down the path towards Lee's house just before you got to the railroad track between our houses. It was slightly hidden in the edge of the woods with lush green bushes over hanging the door or mouth of the lake that we called "the clay hole". Beginning the first day of spring we went swimming every day, and yes, I got a whipping every day. However it never deterred my thinking at all, we got real excited when we watched the summer Olympics on TV, particularly when the swimming events came on. We watched the swim teams who had all white swimmers competing, no blacks.

We saw the white people during the freestyle, butterfly and backstroke with such ease and agility that we convinced ourselves that we could do likewise just like everything else in our lives, if we liked it and believed that we could do it, we went and practiced it until it became naturally easy, we would have conquered the sport.

One day Lee and I were enjoying ourselves during the back stroke and in one motion and stride, flip over into a beautiful freestyle. We had no idea that Dad had sneaked down the embankment from the highway and railroad track and was hiding in the bushes to watch us swim and frolic for quite some time. I heard Dad laughing out loud and praising us for being professionals just like the ones on TV. Dad had only been pretending to be whipping the daylights out of me at the end but not at first. I was pretending also by yelling at the top of my voice in order to calm the nerves of my fearful mother. In my neighborhood as it is in all black neighborhoods in the South, all black parents were intrinsically fearful of any body of water that was larger than a number three tub; We didn't have money to buy toys that we wanted to play with so we used our ingenuity to make what we wanted. We made bows and arrows ourselves by taking a light weight cane stick and placing the cap of a soda bottle at the end and hammering it down around the tip of the stick to make an arrowhead. We used a thick cord type of thread to string our special and unbelievable resilient tree branch from the forest. We would pull the bow to its maximum capacity, hold it for about three seconds and then release the arrow. The arrow would fly so high into the sky that it would go out of sight for a brief moment until it started to descend.

My dad bragged much about the fact that Lee and I were great swimmers around the various communities and Churches and my perseverance would prove to be worth while not many days later.

One day Lee and I were hutting with our bb guns in the woods behind my uncle's house on his farm when we came upon an irrigation pond in a clearing. My uncle's oldest son who was a couple of years younger than we were decided to follow us, he and his two younger brothers. Neither one of them could swim just like everyone in black neighborhoods in those days. Lee and I stood on the banks and looked at the beautiful and calm waves on the wide body of water that were just glittering in the sunlight. Now, Lee and I had never swam in any water deeper than four feet or so, water that we could stand up in if we got tired. We knew that irrigation ponds were about twenty feet deep with a slight slant inward at the edge and then a sudden twenty foot drop straight down!

We were about twelve years old so we were quiet confident in our skills. We peeled off all of our clothing and dove in. I swam out about half the way across the pond and came back. While standing on the bank of the pond I told Lee that this water was much different than the water in the clay hole, it was much clearer and because it was deeper it was much easier to stroke than the clay hole. Unless it rained a lot you could always stand up and rest if you got tired but this water was deeper than I imagined. Standing on the bank looking down into this water with the wind blowing softly, causing gentle waves to appear was very inviting.

I soon discovered that we had made a grave mistake by allowing my younger brother and three young cousins to follow us that day. Of course we couldn't have prevented them from coming along anyway they always followed us if they saw us going to do something interesting and fun.

When I dove back into the water I noticed the softness of it and the easiness of the stroke to carry me through the water was exhilarating! I went down deep towards the bottom but I turned back for it was too deep. On my way out of the water, before I could say or do anything my cousin (Jessie Jr.) alternate name, had taken off all of his clothing and dove into the pond, passing by me as I stood up on the edge.

To my knowledge he had never been in any type of swimming hole before deep or shallow. I rushed up onto the ponds bank so that I could see him and yell at him as soon as he came up to the top! Suddenly one of Jessie's brothers said with a scared voice, Jr. can't swim Arvanie, and he had already been down under for a reasonably long time. Everyone was waiting "anxiously" and with great anticipation! Dad had just bragged about my swimming skills only a few days ago and now there was no time to think about the fact that I had absolutely no rescue experience.

"Suddenly "I heard a familiar small voice from within say, Arvanie, I will be with you always, even to the ends of the earth. Without hesitation I dove in with no ambiguity, right away I saw Jessie Jr. comely and confidently waiting, just stooping slightly on the balls of his feet in a crouching position with one arm outstretched and the other holding his nose. He looked calm and waiting as if he knew that his cousin Arvanie was coming to get him.

As soon as I reached out and grabbed his arm that was extended and began pulling him up I immediately realized that I should have never allowed him to clutch onto my body. I knew that this grip was exactly the kind of grip that I had heard of many times before from the older boys in tobacco and cotton fields, told by people who had seen or heard of someone drowning; As I was making my way back up to the surface of the water Jessie Jr. began hysterically and strenuously fighting to get his head up out of the water so that he could get a breath of fresh air. Air that was greatly needed because he had been under for quite a while.

When his nostrils drew the first breath I could feel his body tighten up around my neck with his arms, and around my waist with his legs and feet. He fought with all of his might to stay up out of the water to keep the precious air coming into his lungs, but at the same time he was pushing me under, denying me the opportunity to receive air also. Suddenly I remembered the story that I had heard about the drowning victims who would reach for a floating match in the water if one came floating by. Now it was I who was looking for that match!

Jessie had latched onto me with both arms and legs tightly wrapped around me and my whole life flashed before my eyes as I was desperately looking for something to grab onto in order to save myself! This was truly the "death grip" and I resigned my mind to the fact that I was going to die, both Jessie and I were as good as gone. But within an instant, without even thinking about Jessie's welfare a powerful thought arose in my mind. If I don't break free, we both were without any doubt going to die, right here, and right now! I remembered the morning in Church while I was teaching Sunday school when the class read in unison the scripture that read, I will be with you always, even to the ends of the earth(Jesus said), after everyone was quiet I heard it again but only in my ear, Arvanie, I will be with you always!

"Suddenly and instinctively" I drew both my knees up into Jessie's body and pushed both my arms up through the inside of his, which were locked around my neck and miraculously I broke free in one quick swift motion. Call it what you will but I knew that the idea came from "God". I was on my way out of the water when I heard the soft voice again, go back and grab Jessie's arm this time and that's just what I did. There was no thinking and no afterthought; I Just did what the voice told me to do and that's how I saved my cousin's life that day. I was not about to let him take a hold of me like he did before.

I had started to swim back to the shore of the pond but I couldn't leave him, I just turned back in one motion, grabbed his arm and pulled him out to safety; Until this day I cannot determine at which point did God intervene or weather he orchestrated the entire incident to test my faith.

Once I got back onto the shore of the pond I begun to recall in silence each segment of the event that had just taken place. I remembered seeing Jesse crouched down on the bottom of the pond holding his nose, and I had never taught him that, he had to have heard it somewhere in small talk somehow, this kid to "my amazement" never panicked until I got his head up above the water level so that he could breathe.

After we gathered our clothing and got dressed, we didn't go straight home, we went to our camp that we had hidden in the woods on my Dad's farm to talk and calm down. We told everyone there that day not to tell anyone about the incident that had just happened for fear that we would never be allowed near any body of water ever again for sure. But by the time I got home I was amazed at all of the fuss that everyone was making, calling me a hero, not just in my home but all over the neighborhood, everyone knew!

At twelve years old I was famous, it was the same feeling that I had in the third grade when I tore into Brown Bomber as if he was a highly favored ice cream cone that everyone wanted with a bright "red cherry" on top, except this time the fame was much greater!

Continuing My Basketball Preparation

Allowing my mind to re-engage in the thoughts and feelings that I had in junior high school, remembering the uncertainty and preparing to fulfill my life long dreams. Consequently I have always been attracted to new ideas and new ways of during the same old things in life. Every day I realized that I was embarking upon new and fresh opportunities to get where I wanted to go. My mind and body was locked on the premise that I was without a doubt going to be a rich businessman someday. I looked at my options and tracks to run on that I could develop and perfect!

I remember reading an article in either the jet or Ebony magazine about a self-made multi-millionaire who started from humble beginnings, and found someone or something to latch onto and use as a goal setting tool to propel him into the next level.

This guy said something that amused and fascinated me greatly. He said that it did not matter much weather you were in sales or service, the most important thing about business was that you must not only be very familiar with your product, you must develop your product knowledge into a science, such that no one knew your product better than yourself!!

I was twelve and the only opportunity and the only product that was available to me was sports, and the only sport at my school was basketball. I began to diligently watch every player on the high school basketball team during practice at recess to determine who brought what to the game, and their roll on the team. Coach practiced basketball every day, all year long. Whenever I saw someone execute a move that I liked, I went home and practiced that move in a pickup game until I perfected it and made it my own move.

Although I was teased and ridiculed ridiculously, the only thing that really mattered to me was that I was adding one more move to my game no matter how long it took. I was determined to be able to play on a professional level, just like the Pro's on TV. I had to be ready when the time came and I was old enough to try out for the varsity team and make it the first time.

I watched college and professional basketball anytime that it came on TV. By the time I reached the ninth grade and begun playing inter-mural sports and competing against other class teams it was evident to everyone in my school that I was going to be a major player in the years to come, without any doubt. It was my way of selecting my tool that would propel me into the business world. Business was going to be my way of helping the large number of poor people in my community by providing decent jobs to the many gifted people who seemingly had no chance or hope to overcome.

Mr. Noben, My elementary school principal who had gotten promoted to my high school at LB high, knew my athletic abilities well and did not hesitate to tell coach Lefton and everyone else that I was an exceptional athlete. While we were in elementary school, each morning and at recess, Mr. Noben coached and called games in all sports, in soft ball he pitched everyday and" Lordy "have mercy he could throw the ball under handed harder than most grownups could throw over handed, and on top of that he was left handed!

Mr. Noben was a very good athlete and he knew and played all sports very well. While we were playing he would not hesitate to embarrass anyone who made mistakes or fumbles during games or practice. Coach Lefton, at LB high was very successful in his efforts, he managed to advance both boys and girls teams to the finals every year. However, the only sport that we played was basketball year in and year out, even during the Summer months when school was out we practiced basketball.

Our coach had two sons who were both exceptional basketball players but unfortunately, the oldest son was killed in a car accident by a motorist from my hometown, coach lived eight miles away in another town. Understandably coach was devastated by the matter so he left LB high for one year to coach at a neighboring school, leaving the coaching job open that year which turned out to be a blessing for me. The new coach was a very fair man, he didn't care which community that you came from, if you could play and contribute to the teams efforts that's all that mattered to him as it should be. Coach Lefton was different, if you were from canary township and went out for the team, you played in front of better players from Rains.

Everyone knew that the boys from Rains were more talented than the boys from any other community and were taller. That's what caused the continuous friction between the boys from Rains and the boys from Conary. (Alternate name).

The new coach Mr. Will (alternate) was a handsome and well-built guy but he did not possess the electric energy that Coach Lefton had. However he did know talent when he saw it. Coach Will's specialty was football, but since the only sport that we had was basketball, both his and my concerns along with everyone else's would be the "almighty basketball".

Up until I was age nine or ten I suffered from asthma, and when I was down with a cold it magnified the intensity of my breathing short comings. I would wake up in the middle of the night as a young toddler, wheezing and struggling to breathe when my loving mother would get up out of bed in the middle of the night, she prepared homemade remedies for me to take. She also rubbed Vicks vapor rub on my chest and neck. Mom stayed up holding me in her arms until my lungs were clear and I could breathe freely. I will never forget her for the caring support that she gave me.

I made a vow to the Lord that I would one day make my mother a rich woman through my athletic ability, as soon as I was able to breathe freely on my own. Basketball would be my catalyst for fame and fortune, and I know that many other kids had the same dream. A propitious feeling comes over me each time that I recall the nights with the asthma attacks and my mom giving me comfort. I believe that it is one of the only times that I actually heard her say that I love you!

Coach Will was phlegmatic to say the least; There was nothing ordinary or prosaic about him. I have always been a pensive thinker with the ability to project myself into my future. I had decided to become the best basketball player in the state of South Carolina, Win a state championship, and go to the university of North Carolina, and onto the NBA! I was in the ninth grade. The previous year at age thirteen my class was privileged to go to the State fair in Columbia SC. For the first time in my life. Columbia is the Capital of South Carolina and located exactly one hundred miles from my hometown.

The night before we were to leave on our journey, while others in my class were planning on which girl or guy they would spend their day with, I was probing the world book encyclopedia at home, learning everything that I could about Columbia! How high it was above sea level? The terrain, lakes and streams in and around the City's structure. The ratio between blacks and whites in the overall population and the blacks who owned their own businesses.

When we got about forty miles away from Columbia we passed through a town called Sumter, with several signs indicating that there was a College there called Morris College! I had never heard of this College and had no idea that one day I would be attending there. When we got on top of the overpass I was able to look down at the surrounding buildings, they were beautiful.

I noticed that the farther we traveled there was a continuous elevation as we climbed through the hills and small mountains. As we got closer to Columbia the more excited I became. A warm and congenial feeling came over me as if I had been here before. I knew without any doubt that one day I would make this place my home. Today I'm happy to say that I made the perfect decision because for well over thirty years now Columbia has been my home. All of the excitement and anticipation that we all had about the State fair was as we approached the opening gates were more than we expected and then some.

But now, getting back to the basketball and practice, I was watching very intensely every move and every play the star players made.

I watched every day at recess in the gym. On Saturday and Sunday after Church I watched the pro. basketball games on TV. I became obsessed with the game and immediately after watching we went out and conducted neighborhood games into the night. Just as all successful people must be in order to attain their goals.

I prayed and begun to feel the closeness that I used to feel when my Mom used to hold me in her arms when consoling me letting me know that everything would be all right whenever I had an asthma attack. The wonderful closeness when she told me that she loved me. With such a confident feeling I knew that God loved me also and he would help me to develop my skills onto flawlessness. I prayed seven days a week and when I wasn't praying, playing or watching on TV, I was lying in bed building images, and developing moves and strategies that could not be defended against.

After watching the moves executed by players that I liked on TV, I would go directly outside while the move was fresh in my mind and practice until I had developed the move into perfection. The next day at school when we played outside, my classmates and others would laugh and say to me, "Arvanie you can't do that", who do you think that you are. I'd say, just watch me! And then I would laugh, ha ha ha!

I was thoroughly and completely impressed with Wilt Chamberlain's finger rolls and dunks. I learned to finger roll perfectly with both my left and right hands. By the time I reached the eleventh grade I was dunking! I learned several moves by the great "Elgin Baylor "and "Earl Monroe". In 1963 and 1964 my classmates couldn't believe it, and on top of that I was from Rains.

It seems that there is almost nothing that you can talk about intelligently without considering race. There was a white phenomenal basketball player who went to the University of North Carolina whom I was completely fascinated with, "Billy Cunningham "the left hander whom I watched and studded more than any other player. B. Cunningham was the greatest left handed ball player that I have ever seen until this day. It took me longer to perfect his relentless movement to the basket from the right hand side of the key. Billy was unstoppable!

I practiced very long hours into the night, and the first thing I did in the morning before I went to school. It seemed awkward and it was very difficult to dribble, penetrate and end the shot left handed.

Serious Thought in a sad way

There was a black woman, middle aged, who lived in our community and managed her husband's cotton crop while he worked on another public job. It wasn't a large crop so she only hired school students to work after school each day so that we could earn some money for the county fair yearly. It was a good source of income in October every year.

Now there was a boy who moved into Rains about the time that I was thirteen or so, and this boy was related to the two most strongest men that I have ever seen and they worked at the cotton gin not far from where the cotton field was. Those men were six foot five and six seven respectively. However this cousin wasn't so lucky as far as height goes, he was short and stubby, about five foot five at best and had huge muscles that seemed as if they didn't belong on his short stubby frame; The boy weighted about two hundred and ten pounds and had been left back several times at his previous schools in Florida. Florida is where he picked fruit and vegetables to help his family put food on the table for his large family.

We'll call this awkward looking boy "TANK"! Tank used every opportunity he could to intimidate every student that he came in contact with, and it didn't matter how old the student was because he was more than likely older. Tank got a job picking cotton right along with the rest of us little children and he used every opportunity to intimidate everyone in that field, except me. No one was allowed to hold a conversation about anything in the field without having interference from Tank. He made a complete nuisance of himself every day. I noticed that he was slow and awkward; He was the kind of guy who lifted weights excessively to build his body to compensate for his shortness. He did the same thing in school, but out here in this field there was no teachers or grownups to complain to, it was just us smaller kids and big short Tank.

I knew that the day would come when Tank would aggravate or challenge me into a boxing match because I was the boxing champion in school. Even though I was uncomfortable and intimidated also with his huge muscles, I knew that the day would come when I would have to stand up to "TANK'. And so it was, one day as soon as we went into the field tank chose me to make an example of and build his reputation at the same time. However, just like I had always done in times of adversity and uncertainty, I told Jesus to please go with me.

When Tank approached me boastfully with his fists balled up and coming straight at me, I went with what I knew and had been taught. If it was inevitable and there was no way out of this fight, I threw a barrage of blows, starting with a strong left jab to the jaw, all in the face. I backed up and looked at him, he was angry and surprised. Before he could throw the right hand that he had cocked, I faked to the stomach and went right back up beside his head, only with four or five slaps this time, nothing was fazing him so, the next thing that I knew that he was too slow to beat me doing was running, so, I took off running as fast as I could and I knew that it was impossible for Tank to catch me.

I had been training with boxing gloves by this stage of my life for a couple of years at least and I was very good. My brother PJ had been training me by holding up both of his hands up beside both sides of his face and my objective was to try and get a punch through to his face without him slapping me in my face. My objective was to develop speed and accuracy along with avoiding getting hit at the same time. By the time Tank came along I was a proficient pugilist(boxer) at a very young age. Practice gave me confidence and once I threw the first punch all fear was gone;

I ran as fast as I could leaving Tank far behind both humiliated and frustrated. Occasionally I turned around laughing and teasing him about his huge and heavy legs, legs that should not be on his body! He was extremely slow in his movements with his feet as well as when he throw punches. You could see his large fists coming as if they were in slow motion. The same thing happened for about two weeks every day, however I underestimated his anger and rage that he kept inside of himself. And little did I know that this beast would ultimately come back to haunt me one day soon;

One beautiful spring morning on the playground at school before the bell sounded for school to open, just as many of us boys who could actually play the game of basketball, we were playing pickup games and the next person in line called rise, indicating that he would have the opportunity to select a team to play the winners. Now, Tank hand been standing around every morning and no one wanted to play with him or against him because he was simply a trouble maker. But this would be the last game that we would have time to play before the bell sounded for our first period class. My team had just lost after a string of wins all morning and Tank chose me because I was thought of as one of the best, which meant that I would make the other selections for the team because everyone wanted to be on my teams. We were playing full court and Tank was really no good at this game and no one would pass him the ball, including me!

Suddenly there was a fast break and I had the ball going down court when I heard Tank continuously calling me for the ball. He was slow getting down court as usual, and he couldn't dribble so I ignored him completely. I took the shot and made the basket, nothing but net. I was on my way back down court when I passed by Tank looking back when suddenly, and right out of the blue, He turned my shoulder and punched me squarely in the mouth. Tank had slipped up behind me and pulled my shoulder around just like we had seen many times on TV when someone was fighting. He folded my two front teeth in slightly and I was bleeding for the first time in my life from a punch. I was caught totally off guard and in shock standing on my feet. Before I had time to think or decide how I would step up with my attack once I recovered from being blindsided, I placed my tongue upward and rolled it across my teeth to feel how badly I was injured. One of the older boys ran over to inspect my injury and determined that I should go quickly to the principal's office so that he could take me to the dentist office.

I had already decided that this was not the time to launch a fighting attack, however, it was the opportunity that I was waiting for to leave the scene without showing any fear, although I wasn't afraid I didn't want to look as if I was afraid to fight. I had determined that when you're already hurt to this extent I didn't care what anyone said, I was concerned about saving my teeth, I could always fight again another day. I simply loved to fight and I knew that I was good at it.

When I got to the principal's office, Mr. Noben examined my injury and said the teeth might have to come out, it was possible that they could be saved. 'Whew "they were calming words and I sat down and relaxed just so that Mr. Noben could start to tease me, he knew my reputation for being a great boxer from elementary school. He said Arvanie when do you think that you will be ready to get him back. I said it might take a while, but in the meantime I'm going to work on building my body and my upper body strength. He said, that's a good idea Arvanie, Tank is nineteen years old, soon to be twenty in a couple of months and he weights over two hundred pounds. You're fourteen and I weighed one thirty five or one forty, it was time to seriously work on my body, and that I did. I immediately started an exercise routine which included two hundred pushups in increments of twenty per set. Numerous setups, jumping jacks, toe touches and one hour plus punching the heavy bag. It took me a year to get ready but everyone refused to have anything to do with Tank after he sucker punched me and he was completely ostricised. When the summer was over and the fall semester started I went looking for Tank, I was ready, I wanted him on the playground so that everyone could me take him apart. It would have to wait, Tank had left the State and gone back to Florida to pick fruit, and stay far away from Arvanie. Just a moment, I'm getting ahead of myself.

After I sat in the Principal's office until my mom came to pick me up to go to the dentist office, I listened to her scold me but showed me sympathy when she found out that it was Tank, the all American bully who had hit me.

When there was silence in the car I began to recall the issues leading up to the point of impact when Tank's fist's connected with my face. The only thing that I could have done differently was to never leave an enemy behind you literally, and never turn your back on a known enemy. I realized that I wasn't big enough to hurt Tank, there was no way to stop him in a fair confrontation. This was not the time to be brave and to stand and fight, I was already injured too severely. Realizing that there was absolutely nothing that I could have done differently, I resolved to communicate silently with my friend and savior Jesus Christ. I said Jesus, I 'am fourteen years old and Tank is nineteen years old, why did this happen to me? You caused me to be born under the number seven and now I have two of them at age fourteen, I expected only good things would happen in my life now. Why have I not only just been embarrassed, I could lose my two front teeth and become toothless for the rest of my life. What lesson am I supposed to learn from this?

I didn't hear the familiar small voice this time but I begun to receive conclusive and definitive thoughts, overwhelmingly! My mind began to communicate to the unknown, the number seven represents avenues of both good and bad, suffering and blessings on the road to perfection and completion.

Suddenly as I was feeling comfort, we approached a stop sign and we saw a white farmer in his blue truck directly in front of us on the other side of the street. This farmer was one that everybody liked to work for, if you finished the work that he wanted in a half day he would pay you for the whole day. He looked at my dilemma and immediately suggested that we go to his dentist. He said that this dentist that he was referring to was very innovative and that he was certain that he could save my teeth. He also went home and called the dentist and made the emergency appointment for me right away. I suddenly began to receive a feeling of certainty and confidence in this dentist before I ever met him.

I continued my serious but sad thoughts and remembering my past obstacles that I had successfully overcome with God's help, in route to the dentist office. First there was "Goldie" and then the little light skinned Goliath and his trick with the right hand lead; Just like Muhammad Ali's right hand lead in Zaire Africa on big George Forman! Those were the bad things but the good things included at age seven, I realized that the only person that I wanted to be like, was to think like the wise King Solomon, not to include the wives. Solomon's army experienced no war during his entire reign of forty years, and most importantly, there was absolutely no hunger in the land and he fed his families well. However I only wanted to be a King in my own household as God ordained. There is no need for a good King to have harsh and will breaking authority over anyone. I had the opportunity to feel and think as a King in the Christmas play, "WE THREE KINGS".

It was a good thing that we met the white farmer in the blue pickup truck on the way to the dentist's office that we knew. We sometimes finished his tobacco by eleven o'clock on Saturday morning and got paid for the day.

So I felt that the good and the bad were the natural vicissitudes of life that we are expected to overcome and go on. Tank was from my home town and students were already segregated by communities from which they lived. Tank wasn't able to make friends with anyone anywhere and when he sneaked me with that punch everyone ostracized him completely. But now seriously, I could lose my teeth and I was uncertain to say the least. I silently asked Jesus, what was I supposed to learn from this? And more importantly I asked him to save my teeth!

It was a miracle! The dentist took one look at my teeth as soon as I sat down in the chair and said with absolute certainty that my teeth were not that bad and that he could surely save them. Both mom and I breathed a sigh of relief, she went into the room with me. This would be my first visit to the dentist and it was a very good experience because in those days, white dentist only pulled black folks teeth, never tried to save any teeth, didn't think that it was important to us.

I knew that Jesus intervened on my behalf. Sadly though the dentist only had a pink hardening mixture to brace my teeth with to sustain my eating habits until my teeth healed well enough to remove the brace. I had to wear a pink brace on my teeth for six weeks which was awkward, but most effective.

My teeth healed perfectly but Tank was ostracized so completely that sadly he dropped out of school over the summer, leaving me without my opportunity to retaliate. I was deeply saddened by that for a long time.

I began to concentrate all of my efforts beyond school work to studying wisdom, and developing my basketball skills.

At age fifteen and in the tenth grade I went out for the basketball team at five foot ten inches tall and made it easily. Coach Lefton was away at another school and the new coach treated me with good admiration and allowed me to assume the role of seventh man but it turned out to be six man on the team in just a short while. I only averaged three or four points per game but I played in every game, just what I needed, experience. I would be ready for business the next and my junior year.

CHAPTER SIX

The HOLY GHOST-HOLY SPIRIT- And first Love

At age sixteen a very denigrating and precarious event occurred at my home Church in Rains. Little did I know that there would be obstacles to overcome in Church. I was attending a special professional gospel singing competition at one of our Sunday evening services along with some local groups as well.

There was the assumptive attitude in the Holiness Churches that when the Holy Ghost came upon you, weather it was as a result of prayer and seeking or going down to the moaning bench, as we called it, the alter prayer. As one chanted certain Jesus phrases, the Holy Ghost seemingly would come down on you, and cause you to jump and shout aimlessly, flinging your arms around in the air, you would then be declared to have received the Holy Ghost.

Repeating phrases or through jubilation and song, and don't forget, someone would come and put their hands on your head as if they were assisting God in giving you the Holy Ghost as soon as they saw you perhaps getting in the spirit. There would be singing and shouting all over the Church; This behavior was expected of you if you wanted to belong to the group of saved individuals. Consequently there would be many who would fake the behavior after attaining a certain age in order to be accepted into various Church organizations.

A very good group began to sing a powerful and beautiful song that moved me, and suddenly, as if someone just lifted me up right out of my seat, I found myself not only standing but I was intensely listing to the voice say, go, for now is the time. Normally when I felt the presence of the Lord upon me I would hurriedly get up out of my seat and go quickly outside before anything else happened, and have a private talk with Jesus alone. I told Jesus many times that I absolutely had no desire to jump and shout, I wanted to be a mighty man of valor and it just didn't look right for a macho man like myself to jump and shout all over the place, that's for wimps and it's too embarrassing! The Holy Spirit spoke to my mind and I heard it loud and clear in my ear. God would not put anything on me or cause me do anything that was not placed within my character spirit before I was ever born. Seemingly I felt safe from the embarrassment of shouting in public. But now our Pastor came down from the pulpit and stood in front of the alter and said, the doors of the Church are open, who so ever will let him come. He was looking directly at me and didn't turn to anyone else at all. He knew that I had received a call to join the Church and give my life to the Lord.

I found myself walking towards the alter and standing before the Church and the Pastor. This was the last song in the program and as our pastor always did, he extended the invitation to everyone in the church, but I was the only one that he was looking at, and the only one to step out, no one ever tried to join our church without first jumping, shouting and screaming all over the place. I was the only one to step out; I had observed many times before in church services when the presence of the Holy Spirit was moving in the church there would be shouting and dancing for the Lord, but only by the women. There was one man however who would occasionally burst into a shouting episode. My brother Billy on many occasions went down to the alter to be prayed for in prayer meetings seeking the Holy Ghost but in those days I don't believe that many candidates really knew how to ask to be set free from sin.

Asking the Lord to come into their lives and take full control. I was empathetic towards Billy because he never did receive the Holy

Ghost by going down and have the saints pray over him and pressing their hands on his head while he sat there. He received it in later years while he was alone. He never faked it and I was proud of him for that.

I was not ready to submit my whole life to Christ and live a Christian life as I perceived. I was only sixteen years old and my body was in great athletic condition. I was now six feet tall, one hundred and eighty eight pounds in the eleventh grade and I wanted to experiment with alcohol like the big boys did, and I was not willing to give up my opportunity to experience the companionship of the pretty girls sexually. Speaking in tongues was another aspect of showing the evidence of receiving the Holy Spirit, or under the influence of the Holy Ghost.

Sadly, some people, once they had observed enough of the varying attributes or functions and performances of showing evidence of having received the Holy Ghost Sunday after Sunday, they would periodically get up, jump and shout, recanting and reciting a few variations of words that they had heard someone say and duplicate them in order to acquire status in the church. When the Holy Spirit urged me to go forward I stepped out of the pew and found myself being greeted by the pastor. Now, I never would have expected what was about to happen to me in a thousand years; My pastor was happy to see me come forward, I had been teaching Sunday school all of my life in this church and I was the first in many years to come up to join the church in a long time. No one new ever joined our church. In fact I had never witnessed anyone join our church and here I was, the first one to try to join without having showed any evidence of the Holy Ghost.

I thought that I would be surely welcomed and surely be given the right hand of fellowship. But to my surprise low and behold, when the pastor announced me as a candidate for baptism and to become a full member of Hope church, the church that I had spent my entire life worshiping in along with my parents and grandparents, teaching both junior and young adult Sunday school classes from age seven to that present day, My own uncle who was the superintendent with a lot of power in the church and the only one to object to or say anything for that matter. He stood up and said the church would not accept the young man Arvanie Graves into the church today, I don't believe that he is quiet ready. Until this day I don't know if he thought that the only way to be accepted into the church or if the only way to be accepted by Jesus is to display evidence of having received the Holy Ghost, weather you fake it or not to prove it to man;

Now listen, I was just sitting enjoying the services and periodically thinking about going home after church to prepare for my Sunday night's date. A date that I always looked forward to with a beautiful young girl indeed. And now here I was, standing in front of the whole church for I don't know how long, waiting for what seemed like an eternity for the words to come from someone in the church to say, let's make an exception in this case, we know that he loves both the Lord and the church, and besides he is an example for the young people, he is the Sunday school teacher. No one even got up to say on my behalf, let's make Arvanie a trial member for a short period; I was totally embarrassed and all eyes were on me. Nothing like this had ever happened to anyone in this church before and trust me, it never will again because unless the next candidate is prepared to fake the matter brilliantly, no one will ever attempt to join Hope church again!

I felt as though the leaders of the church failed badly that day. Not only was this the church that my Grandfather hope to build with his money and his own hands, I felt that they had somehow dis-embodied me from the church both physically and spiritually. I thought that they had separated me from the promises of Jesus Christ for a while. The Deacons of the church began to whisper as to their incompetence which flowed throughout the church. The pastor waited patiently and embarrassed as well at the ignorant denial but the words of acceptance never came. I was humiliated, disappointed, saddened with a strong feeling of rejection that I had never experienced before. I looked into the pastor's sad hurtful eyes and turned and walked away, all the way out of the church! I turned and looked into my mother's eyes, she was sobbing intensely as I did what I always did when I was hurt and alone. I began talking to God as if he was right there with me, to try and find some form of comfort.

I felt that the church leaders had failed God's purpose and me, all in one brief ignorant act. It would be years later before I felt completely reunited with my Lord and savior Jesus Christ. I also made the decision that day that as soon as I was old enough, I would detach myself, not only from this holiness Church but all Holiness churches in the entire world!

Mom and the ladies of the church turned over a new leaf that day, they actually stood up to the Deacons and other men of the Church that day on my behalf. They stayed for hours after church to find a solution to that problem. They deliberated until after four o'clock that Sunday on options to deal with my circumstance, and with Mom's persuasion they decided to except me under a Christian experience, but the men won the decision to not allow me to be baptized at this time. The women did get the men to agree to start a prayer roll on my behalf. It really didn't matter to me though I was through with the Holiness Church forever!

Sadly though, some of the people who practiced faking having received the Holy Spirit in Churches before men to gain status in the Church are still faking it today; I realized that once you fake having the Holy Ghost in Church it becomes too difficult to come again a year or so later and say, well, I didn't really get filled with the Holy Ghost back then so I want to try and get it for real now. Most saints will declare that you are a terrible sinner with a demon upon you, or what makes this time any different for anyone to believe you now as opposed the time before.

IN LOVE, THE VERY FIRST TIME

What is love that we should acknowledge thou? Essentially I began to work on my vocabulary when I enrolled In Morris College the second semester in the year 1967. I took grammar 101 under the auspices of Dr. W. Brown, who was an accomplished and former writer of scripts for the (Alfred Hitchcock) show, the twilight Zone and other TV features in the sixties era.

I have found and determined that the word "love" is a word of infinity boundless and the most powerful emotion in the universe; This is something that's worth repeating in my opinion. Neurologist, Dr.'s who study the human brain and the capabilities of the mind, have discovered and determined that the human mind produces over sixty thousand thoughts every twenty four hours. Thought that are measured by dendrites, that can only be seen under a microscope as being seven times smaller than a period at the end of a sentence....... The problem is that we think the same thoughts every day, who we will date, what car should I buy to define me? High gas prices, what about lunch, dinner and supper?

When I came upon the realization that I was thinking the very same thoughts each and every day, I made a graphic change in my mental behavior. I sought out and investigated the art of "Meditation".

When I was introduced and came upon the emotion of love for the very first time, I was fifteen years old and in the tenth grade of high school. My mind and heart immediately carries me back to the spring of 1965. I was in the homeroom class of my older sister whom we will call (Mildred). Mildred was a tall dark and beautiful girl who was the first female in our hometown to ever go to college. She blazed an enormously wide trail as far as studies and awards for accomplishments go.

It was a beautiful time and season of the year, the air is overflowing with elegant fragrances and sweet smelling odors and savors blowing in the wind from both near and far; Students began to wear cooler clothing which exposed slightly more flesh and curves, un ha-breast "ooh wee". The young girls were beginning to bud and flower and my thoughts were breath taking! Life itself was young and beautiful and everything seemed exciting, and I knew that my life was just beginning, nothing should go wrong, it should only go wright;

In the spring time of each year every homeroom teacher was assigned the task of putting together either a mayday dance or play competition, whichever the majority of the class could agree on. Our class decided that we would do a dance so my sister let the class decide what type of music that we would dance to. No one even had a clue as to what type of music or dance that we could all dance to competitively except (alternate name) Lil Bill Tee, who turned out to be my cousin that I was not aware of at the time.

Lil Bill Tee said, I know a record that would be perfect and we could possibly win the May Day dance competition of the entire school with; I learned as we all did very soon that Lil Bill Tee had not only an ear for music, he had planning and directing skills as well. The song that he chose was "HOT CHOW", BY Jr. Walker and boy was it beautiful. My sister Mildred began to pair us off as dance partners who she thought could dance well together and who would have thought that she would chose for my partner the beautiful (alternate name) Lisa Tee, Lil Bill's sister, the most beautiful girl in the entire school, except one who was equally as beautiful, the mesmerizing L.H., the girl with the Indian sounding name.

Lisa and I danced every day to the melodic beautiful and energetic sounds of Jr. Walker's horn. As I held Lisa close to me several times a day every day and moved brilliantly across the floor she followed and we connected perfectly. Moving and grooving loosely as we strolled across the dance floor to the new rendition of the two step that Lisa and I developed, a soft close shag- Fred Astaire combined with our own movements. Trust me, we danced so good together that we won the dance competition and we were chosen to be "KING and Queen" of the school competition of 1965.

Lisa was very accentuating in that she danced with such ease an agility that she complimented my movements quite well. As we danced daily for practice we both grew fond of each other and pretty soon we fell in love and were dating.

So, the night of the big dance Lisa and I were the first in line to lead the procession out onto the dance floor and we were waiting for Lil Bill to start the music. Everyone was nervous except Lisa and I. I actually felt like this was what I was born to do, lead and accomplish. I was in my rightful place, what could go wrong. When I'm prepared it gives me great confidence and I was rearing to go, not to mention that I have great love for showing off when it is something that I am good at doing! When the music started with Jr. Walker started blowing his horn to the tune of "hot chow "I gently placed my right arm around Lisa's waist and we strolled out onto the gymnasium floor, the stadium was packed. We commenced to take the show into our own hands and with the grace and pride of champions!

We both quickly realized that there was way too much saw dust on the already shinny slippery floor which speeded up our step as we turned the corner. The turn caused Lisa's queen's crown to fall from her head to the floor as she slightly lost her footing but I held her tightly in my arms momentarily as she regained her footing! Although I realized that the proper gentlemanly thing for me to do was to stop, stoop down and pick up the crown and put it back on her head properly but, --"but it was 1965" and I am always thinking and re-thinking, and I am nobody's dummy. I was a good looking sixteen year old boy with a cool black tux with tails on, dancing with the prettiest girl in the entire school.

My mom had just bought me a beautiful burgundy star chief Pontiac, long, with sun visors and a cool white top, just so that I could drive it to the prom that year.

Everything was just right, now all that I needed to do was to reach down to pick up the crown and slip and loose my footing and hit the floor with everybody in the gym looking. I knew that anything that could go wrong on a perfect night like this, would go wrong. So I looked into Lisa's eyes and smiled and she smiled back, a meeting of the minds so to speak, "oh no" just leave it where it is and continue dancing and control the flow of the evening! We both had the same premonition of me reaching down to pick up the crown, slipping on the saw dust and the whole gym full of people laughing at me! Someone else picked it up for us and everything went just as our entire class had predicted. We won and there was a ceremony celebrating our victory.

I didn't tell anyone what was on my mind afterwards but I realized that this was the second time in my life that I was though of and was called a "king". Lisa and I dated regularly until sister Mildred went home and told mom who I was dating and when I came home from school that afternoon we had a family meeting, just mom and me. Mom hesitantly told me that Lisa was my second cousin. My Granddad and Lisa's mother were brother and sister, no one in our entire family had ever heard Lisa's mother's name mentioned in my whole life. Including my sister Mildred. Needless to say, I was crushed, now how can this be. So I asked mom very dejectedly, are you certain? I waited for the wrong answer to come out right somehow. The only thing that I was interested in hearing at that moment was no son, I was just joking, but that answer never came. Mom calmly looked into my eyes and said reluctantly, yes Arvanie, she is your cousin;

I went outside to my quiet place behind our barn and just stood there quietly for many moments just thinking. I thought about all of the good clean fun that we had with each other. Sitting and talking on her mom's couch about unimportant things, laughing and enjoying each other's company. We talked on the phone for hours every night. I was in love for the first time in my life which was over and above a crush and there was no question that this feeling was different from the crush that I encountered in the third grade, nothing ever felt like this before. It was painful buy I wasn't experiencing any physical pain. I was saddened for loosing someone that I had not totally lost yet. I was confused because it happened just as abruptly as it had when I discovered that I was in love however the falling was a gradual process that slipped up on me. It was embarrassing and yet I wasn't really embarrassed. I think all of the time and now I was confused as to how could I fall in love and not know that I would have to end the relationship abruptly. For several hours Lisa was the only thing that I could think of and I would have to bring this same uncomfortable feeling upon her because I knew she felt the same way that I did.

That night I went out behind the barn again and looked at the beautiful dark sky with all of the millions of beautiful stars, there were no street lights in most country Towns and communities in the sixties so I could see how softly God had sprinkled the millions of beautiful and extremely bright stars against the rich black and beautiful sky! I looked and meditated for a long time, I was looking for God to come into view and come close in any shape or form that he chose to. I ask Jesus, what did you mean? When you said that you would be with me always. Suddenly the thought came to me and I heard the remnants of that thought in my own voice, yes Arvanie, I'm here and I feel that same pain, it is only another obstacle that you must overcome on your journey.

Here I was, a six foot tall good looking boy with the most beautiful 1960 burgundy with a white top Pontiac star chief car, the best looking car in town for miles around, I was dating the most beautiful girl in our school, however suddenly unlike any other thought that I had ever entertained before, the beautiful girl with the "Indian sounding name", she would become my next girlfriend I thought, and I began to feel better momentarily.

I was on the basketball team and headed in the direction that I had planned all of my life and only a few hours ago I was the happiest kid that I knew, and now I would have to tell Lisa.

I knew that I had had some sensational dreams about my future and they were at the forefront of my mind, God's calling and purpose for my life. Up until now Lisa and I had dated on her mom's couch in her living room so I thought that it would be best if we went out to see a movie, and later I would tell her under a moonlit sky, it seemed easier under the moonlight.

We went to a movie that night an afterwards I drove the big beautiful Star Chief Pontiac onto the campus of my elementary and middle school athletic field where I used play as a running back in football, and I played short stop and second base in baseball. The night was calm and very quiet. I leaned over and kissed Lisa, and I told her before things went any further, Lisa, this might come as a shock to you but it's been on my mind now for almost a week. What, she said? I hesitated for a moment as I looked into her compassionate lovely eyes, mom said that we were cousins, that my Grandfather and your mother are certainly brother and sister. We are second cousins but this hold thing is confusing to me. Lisa looked at me with an unusually calm demeanor on her face and then she said Arvanie I already knew that; she told me that her mom had already told her the same thing but that it was too late, because she was in love also!

When I took Lisa home I went inside to talk to her mom and she confirmed to us that we were indeed second cousins. I wondered, no one had ever mentioned this to us. When I left that night I told Lisa that I wouldn't be back but I realized right away that it would be the most difficult thing that I would ever have to do in life but I found out that I was going to face a greater hurt involving another cousin of an entirely different circumstance; I swaggered around for many days, pretending that I was cool with the breakup but I was a complete sorrowful mess! Happily though it was during the summer now and school was out. I didn't have to see Lisa everyday and trust me, that was truly a lifesaving blessing for the both of us. My sister teased me quite a bit but I'm sure that she didn't know how badly that I was feeling. The pain was so great until I waited before I decided to date anyone else. I thought well, God must not intend for anyone to have a successful relationship with their first love…The pain is designed to cause so much irritability and discomfort that one will be careful about whom you give your heart to, and to seriously take many things under consideration before you select a wife or husband.

One day I realized that there was only one person that I could talk to who could surely tell me how to overcome the pain of love. That person was my cousin and also my Agriculture teacher who lived just across the field from us, I called him "Fess" short for Professor or Wiseman!

Fess had been my mentor since grade school so I knew that I could trust him and his judgment. Fess taught us much more than how to grow cabbage, he taught us how to be responsible young men. If you were going to drink alcohol he made sure that you realized that to become a drunk was not only distasteful, it was life's greatest disaster for anyone who had intentions of going somewhere in life. Fess was the first successful businessman that I had ever come in contact with and if there was anything that you needed to know, Fess was the man with the answer.

King Solomon said that Wisdom was the greatest thing, and that you must search for it as if it was pure "Gold". To memorize scripture and other historical facts causes man to consider you smart, however when you gain the ability to receive Knowledge and to determine how it applies to the natural order of things, and if you encounter a problem that you cannot solve, but you know where and to whom to go and see to find the answer, takes wisdom;

If lighting strikes a tall tree in the woods it might take several months or even a year perhaps for the tree to completely die and fall to the ground and there it will lie. However if you re-visit that tree and roll it over you will find all kinds of new insect life existing and habitating which rids the earth of other unwanted pest and new growth will appear.

Now back to my love pain, Fess told me as we walked through his beautiful garden which always looks as if someone had drawn the vegetables in a picture book. He told me that the only way to avoid another broken heart, and to live through long periods of time thinking and feeling uncertain, is to date many girls at the same time. There would be a danger of fathering many illegitimate children if you are not careful, but it is difficult to be in love with more than one woman at the same time. It is not fair to the young ladies but it will protect "your heart".

CHAPTER SEVEN

"Sabotaged"

Walking away from the one that you love is truly difficult, but walking away from love itself, who has the answer?

The rest of that summer before entering the eleventh grade I was excited and full of great expectations. "Great' is indeed the operative word that consumed me and my expectations for the rest of my days until the present. I had played successfully on the basketball team in the tenth grade under Coach Will and he was impressed with my skills, not only in basketball but many other sports that he had the opportunity to observe me play also. He saw the greatness in my boxing skills and he seriously tried to get me to go into pro-boxing. He also saw me play football and baseball around town in league sports and was very proud and happy to have been my coach. He talked to me a lot about the opportunities that would be available to me at larger schools and colleges.

He was saddened that LB High had previously discontinued the sport of football and baseball, sports that he had excelled in- in college. I was seriously looking forward to getting back to school to see him but it wasn't going to happen, fate steeped in and coach Lefton decided to come back and claim his old job. I practiced and practiced until there was nothing unfamiliar to me about basketball, our only school team sport. I was a player already on the professional level. a combination of several pro players including my own special moves that I had developed in my mind while lying in bed at night, and the next day I would practice those moves into perfection and greatness! I developed Billy Cunningham's left handed penetration to the basket from either side of the basket, I also developed an average left handed jumper. I was executing Wilt Chamberlain's finger rolls with both hands perfectly. Sometimes while approaching the basket I would tuck the ball slightly under my opposite arm as if I was taking the ball from my inside suit coat pocket and finish with the smooth layup finger roll. At 6'00 feet I was dunking the ball easily and the only one on the team that could.

Hesitating jumpers, quick stop pull up jumpers, jumpers off of the dribble from either direction, turnaround jumpers, fade away jumpers and jump flip shots with the wrist only from either side and eight to ten feet from the key over any defenders head, regardless of his height. I had developed so many moves until once I started my approach to the basket, I didn't need a half step, I only needed a lean to beat the defender. Believe me, I would give ten years of my life if I had some film of those years.

This would be the year that Coach Lefton would return to our school and brought with him his youngest son "scoop"(alternative name) who was a spectacular ball player and ball handler. Within a few days after Coach Lefton returned the announcement was made over the public address system(PA), as I mentioned previously, Coach practiced basketball all year, unlike other schools who were blessed to have multiple sports programs in place. We practiced every day during recess and after school which means that we went through the usual cutting and eliminating process of players who didn't make the cut. At recess I had the support and admiration of the entire school. The students were amazed to be able to see moves of professional basketball players right there on our open court every day and I was more than happy to oblige.

This was my opportunity to become famous by having students go back to their neighborhoods and talk to family and friends such that I could be propelled into a scholarship to the famous University of North Carolina.

During our practice sessions after school we got down to business, the first five players from the year before mainly seniors, against myself and the best players left would always play the school team. We managed to win against the school teams first five players as much as we lost, so it was a tossup coach said as to which team he would send in any given game first. Players were making shots and when they executed a move that they thought was good they would cut their eye over at coach to see if he was looking, which seemed to be very elementary to me, that's what coach was there for. I never once looked over at coach, I was confident and prepared. There was no weak points in my game so I was ready to get it on, I needed to get on to the next level of my dream.

After about two weeks of showing coach everything that we had the day came when coach blew the whistle and came out on the floor and called the names of fifteen potential players who had made his team. The rest were asked to leave the Gym. To my surprise coach called my name and my name only and said "Arvanie Graves" you are the first and only player who has made this team so far, you may go over to the stage where he had laid out all of the team numbers and suit uniforms, you may take your pick of any number that you desire! No one else has come close to making my team yet, you're the only one who has made the starting five on this team and the most prepared player that I've seen in a long time. All other players from now on, you will be training for your position on this team. Arvanie Graves has earned his spot on the first string!

Coach continued with his introductory speech by telling all of us that team work and preparedness was the most important thing that he was looking for and Arvanie Graves is the most prepared and developed player in this State today. I know that he has worked hard over the summer and I'm glad to welcome him aboard the "LB wildcats team", everyone else has some serious work to do. Naturally I was "shocked" but not surprised. The players from the first string team from last year were just standing there looking at me with both "envy and surprise" on their faces. At my school we were separated by the different communities that we lived. Naturally the students who came from the town of Canary, the community that our school, LB. high located in, those students were shown favor by coach. The Students from Rains were often ridiculed by coach but the one thing that Coach or no one else could over look was that God had surely shown favor to the people of Rains when he was passing out athletic ability; Both men and women from Rains simply had God given talent in many sports.

So, we were separated but when it came to playing basketball we all were more than happy to come together because it was entirely the only thing that we had as far as entertainment or something meaningful to do. When coach left our school for that one year he took his two sons with him so that he would have the opportunity to coach both sons at the same time. The eldest son, (alternate) QB was a gifted and phenomenal athlete. I mean he had it going on in all sports and coach reflected his complete satisfaction with his ability, who wouldn't be? Well, unfortunately, and I do mean with sincere regrets because I admired him as well.

One Christmas eve QB, coach's oldest son was killed in a head on collision on a country road not far from where coach lived. He was killed instantly by a drunk driver from my hometown, and that drunk driver was my cousin whom I didn't know of our family relationship at the time. That's a serious matter that would come back to haunt me among other things. As fate would have it, coach's youngest son's life would be claimed by that same road about twenty years later, but right now though this was 1965 and my junior year in high school. I'm on the basketball team of a coach with the best win record in our conference for many years.

When coach congratulated me that day on the Gym floor it made me the happiest young man on earth. However I couldn't say with absolute certainty but in my mind back then and it still haunts me today. I thought that I was being rewarded for putting in all of the hard work and training to be an exceptional athlete but instead, I was being set up by my coach, "SABOTAGED", set up to fail without any doubt! It is the one and only obstacle that I have not been able to completely overcome. And now that I am in my late fifties I'm still reminded of those feelings every time I think about my past, even though I have forgiven coach long ago. In my mind I was on track for the completion of reaching the goals that I sat for myself back in grade school. I was truly happy and content; I was being rewarded for working hard and focusing on my goals, I had my uniform for the second year all alone this time for about two weeks before anyone else was allowed to pick a uniform for making the team. That would be a first string player from Canary who was allowed to pick a suit and he had played for a couple of years previously. And so it went day after day until the other four starters were picked from the previous year.

It never occurred to me that coach could be as vindictive as to take out his vengeance on me, a sixteen year old naïve, young and dumb is a better example of my thought processes on this matter; I never thought much about the fact that coach never talked to me personally about anything; Never, never, never once did he mention anything to me about my place in the lineup, nor what was expected of me as a player, no assignment if you will. I just assumed that he felt like there was nothing that I needed to change about my game, he said that I was the best in the State.

I would find out the very first night which was at home court. We all ran out onto the Gym floor and gathered around coach for a last minute pep talk. Coach didn't look up at us that night, he just begun to call out the names of the starting lineup.(alternate names) Ben, Troy, Bill TEE,- a hesitation briefly, and Scoop! his son. Everyone on the team including all of the student fans and their parents were just as surprised as I was, and everyone looked directly at me as if to say coach must be saving Arvanie Graves for our secret weapon! Some of the guys gave me a pat on the butt with a look of assurance to mean that this lineup would only be temporary. Every day at recess we practiced and the entire school watched coach give me the first pick for my team who always won by the way. But tonight, at our very first game where I had planned to establish my superiority as a player, had already played this game many times in my head while lying in bed at night, and here I was sitting on the bench. Coach didn't even look at me the entire night. My heart was broken, I was embarrassed, humiliated and confused. I stuck my chest out with an appearance of confidence that I would get a chance to show my stuff the next game, but that game and opportunity never came.

I was at the beginning of my nefarious education on being discriminated against by darker skinned people as opposed to lighter skinned folks. Coach Lefton was a sharp, neatly dressed individual and he required all of us players to do the same. We were required to purchase a burgundy blazer along with two pairs of dress trousers. One black pair and a grey pair also, accompanied by a yellow shirt and a blue one also. We all had to have white all-star snickers and only white socks at all times. When we walked into an opponent's Gym we all looked like wall street businessmen; Businessman, that's what it was all about for me, to look like, act like, walk and talk like a businessman!

That's what my entire life was all about, establish my name and game in high school, and then onto the University of NC. and onto the Pro's. It didn't matter to me weather I played In a couple of games or two or three years, all that mattered to me was that I stayed long enough to establish my number (30) in the professional league, compete against the best players in the world so that I could market my number as my business name in anything that I chose to market as a product.

Our uniforms were Kelly green and white and they were only two years old. When the buzzer sounded to end the girls game at an opposing team's gym, we had walked in earlier dressed in yellow shirts, black pants and burgundy blazers with black shinny shoes. We carried our gym bags like briefcases. We were intimidating for sure! But now it was game time again and we ran out onto the floor like "mighty warriors" indeed. Great men of valor, I was both mentally and physically prepared even though coach didn't even bother to explain to us why I sat out the entire first game. We respected all of his decisions, he held all of our athletic futures entirely in his hands, who was going to question the great "coach Lefton"! When we went into the huddle we heard these words loud and clear during every break "who are we"— "Wildcats", and coach proceeded to call out the first five, we were all expecting the lineup to change for sure but sadly, it was an exact replica of the first game, no Arvanie Graves the entire game. It saddens me even now when I write these words. No one could have begun to tell me that a grown and wise man so I thought, would treat a vulnerable kid like myself like a complete stranger to our team. In a hundred years I could never prepare myself for that kind of treatment, knowing it in advance. The fans from my hometown and others who had heard about me began to hum and haa with great disappointment. Everyone from miles around had heard about the gifted and talented Arvanie Graves and they had come to see some unusual and spectacular moves on the court, but coach was winning as usual with whomever he sent into the games, to exclude me. Each night we exclaimed proudly, "Wildcats", but when the starting buzzer sounded, it was always without me.

I continued to take my seat on the bench with the chumps and around the fifth home game I resolved to go down as far as I could get away from coach. Sitting on the bench I noticed the time clock registered 30' seconds to go before the half when suddenly, Coach called my name to go into the game. We were leading the other team by twenty points. I went into the game and as soon as I ran to the opposite end of the court, coach called time, and pulled me out of the game with 15 seconds left in the half.

The light finally came on in my head, seven times brighter than the lights in the gym, I was without any doubt, being "sabotaged", set up to surely fail, and everyone in the gym knew it, and sadly, there was absolutely nothing that I could do about it. The great coach Lefton that everyone revered was deliberately causing the fans and student body, but most of all he caused my team mates to feel that he didn't trust me on the court, not even for 15 seconds and with a twenty point lead on the other team. Sadly, I later concluded that was a magnificent didactic methodical approach to tear down an individual's "CONFIDENCE". The five players just stood there for a moment looking confused and dumbfounded, as I was every night for the rest of the entire season. Coach began to overlook me from then on, even after the games were surely in the bag.

Coach would send in players who were clearly, and everyone knew they were inferior players to me. I could not understand how an adult in authority whom everyone actually admired and revered as both a man and a coach could mentally abuse a kid who was humble and my love for the game transcended love, I was hooked on being "great". I was willing to do anything that coach would have asked me to do just to play ball. Coach had methodically destroyed the seconded most important thing that I needed in my life, my confidence.

I didn't quit but I wanted him to cut me as a player so that I could live the rest of my life knowing that I used all of the opportunities afforded me to exhaust all of my possibilities to transfer to another school, but it didn't happen, I had to suffer the humiliation every night on the bench, and riding home on the bus sitting quietly while everyone else was whooping it up to no end. During the entire two years that I played under coach Lefton, he never as much as called me over to the side to talk to me about anything. At the beginning of the season when he called my name to say that I was the best player in the State, and to go pick out my uniform, he was talking about me, not even making eye contact because he knew that he was going to erase my abilities completely, without even laying a finger on me. He never even took the time to say to me, Arvanie, I don't need you right now, he never said a word and didn't look in my direction either.

I was crushed, my dreams were slowly being deleted before my eyes and I was helpless to do anything about it. I knew what it felt like to be raped, and have no one to talk to. I had played more minutes in the tenth grade under coach Will in one "game" than I played under coach Lefton the entire two years.

I wanted to tell coach that I wasn't the one driving the car that killed his beloved "son". As a sophomore I played in every game at age fifteen under coach Will, many nights I wished that it was he coaching us now.

As a sophomore, under coach Will I also took a physical education class and he taught me many things, we talked, he told me how to build my body without gaining the bulk that weights put on you. One day he showed up with a pair of boxing gloves. He paired us off by weight and height and I was matched up with the strongest boy in our class, and he was built to boot. His name was "Lazzo" we were a perfect match though I thought, taking into account my boxing skills. My muscles didn't show as much but I worked out all of the time, in perfect shape. I had been trained in boxing gloves since my grade school days, and this was the opportunity that I was looking for since "Tank" had skipped out on me. This would be the day that I would get a chance to prove that Arvanie Graves was no coward, not by a long shot, I loved to fight! Tank had left me hanging since the incident on the playground with the lucky punch. Lazzo and I were strapped up, ready to do battle, we were the first to step into the squared circle. Just before I stepped into that circle I took a good look at Lazzo, he was way too confident, he thought that I was a coward and he had never been beaten. No one had ever come close to beating him. He was looking at his circle of friends smiling and winking his eye with assurance. I knew how to take his power immediately by showing him some power of my own, I would let him feel my power! I knew that the weight of the gloves would tire him out quickly if he wasn't familiar with them, wear him down over time, three, three minute rounds. My laces were tied and we didn't have any head gear so I stepped right up to him, squared off, gave him a fake as if I was going to the body with a left hook and "wham" I changed direction in one motion and threw a Sharpe and explosive straight jab to the nose and mouth. He was shocked, and gave me a look of surprise but at the same time he was letting me know that he had come to fight also. I followed up with a head fake to the head again and he threw up both hands to cover up but I threw the left hook to the rib cage this time and doubled to the right side of the head. It was 'beautiful" I felt the power leave my body and connect with his head" whap-wham", and put my dukes up to cover my face when he decided to throw punches. I was taught to avoid being caught off guard by any punches thrown, and defray the impact by blocking. Lazzo was tough, he was hurt but not overwhelmed. He came back firing bombs as hard as he could, I was both surprised and impressed, he knew how to throw straight punches, rather than round house blows wildly!

We were equally matched as far as size and punching power but I had much much more experience, moves, and the ability to think on my feet. Considerably more weapons, but as far as pure power and will, we were equally matched and we both quickly knew it. This match was going to be won by points connected and scored. I made sure that he didn't get off but two punches per interval before I broke the barrage by firing off combinations to the head and body. The match was so close that no one at first wanted to call it either way until coach Will said that I won by a nose; Afterwards coach ask me to stop by his office the next morning early. When I did he told me that he used to box and that I was ready to go pro-boxing right away, that I didn't need much training, just a few pointers here and there and I could be a number one contender in no time.

I said no sir to myself, Muhammad Ali was the champ and it wouldn't be long before big George Forman showed up! Lazzo and I immediately became very good friends directly after the boxing match.

we both became famous in the sport of boxing once again, we had both been thinking that we were the best in the school but we found out that it could have easily gone either way.

Lazzo had a huge chest and large forearms, he moved his head from side to side but when I timed him and threw the explosive Vesuvius jab, it stunned and shocked him to the point that he had to change his mind and his game plan altogether. It didn't matter though how hard I hit Lazzo, he just shook it off and kept coming! At one point during the match I had to just smile at his courage, persistence and his ability to take a punch. I was just the opposite, I chose to stick and move to avoid being hit. I made sure that every time that I hit him he would feel my" power"!

The tenth grade is the most fun and memorable year that I had in high school, and if I could I would delete my entire eleventh and senior year, that's exactly what Coach Lefton did to my basketball career; Consecutively delete those two years from my mind completely. That boxing match is still being talked about today, forty years after the fact, but I'm still being haunted by the mental anguish that I suffered under coach Lefton. Several of the older ball players from Rains told me that many of them were treated similarly but nothing could compare with my dilemma and ill treatment. My younger brother had a tremendous ability to rebound and bang the boards, and my baby sister was tall and athletically gifted also but after they witnesses what Coach did to me they didn't play.

At the end of my senior year we had lost the championships both years and you would not believe what happened at the end of the season? The only time that coach had ever spoken to me personally was the very next day after they lost our final game in 1966, Coach Lefton walked up to me while I was leaving the gym for my fifth period class, (after recess) he blocked the door entrance and looked me squarely in my eyes and said these exact words!

"Arvanie", you are only seventeen years old and no one is going to give you a job until you reach eighteen years of age". (Son, you should come back next year and play guard and forward with my son SCOOP)!. I just looked at him with horrific pain in my mind and my heart! As I walked away I realized that my right hand was experiencing a clinched fist on it's own! When I got home I went back behind our barn and looked into the heavens and asked God, exactly what did you mean when you said that you would be with me always? Many times while I was sitting on the bench I was –you guessed it – daydreaming. Dreaming of other places that I wanted to be. King Solomon said that when you're dead, you cannot even think a good thought, so I begun to imagine myself being in New York on Wall Street, dressed in a new suit with my briefcase in hand, looking for the perfect office that I should hold. The Gymnasium would become my market place with all of my clientele sitting in the bleachers, and walking to and fro. There would be instances when other players sitting next to me would have to nudge me really hard to inform me that coach had called my name, and to get ready to go into the game for my occasional less than a minute appearance in the game.

My confidence level had gone down so low that there were times when someone passed me the ball and I would fumble a simple pass! I wanted to be off of that team and to get far away from coach Lefton but there was absolutely nothing else to do in school or the entire County for that matter. My life seemed useless and boring, I could see why kids committed suicide, however when it crossed my mind the thought did not surface; It didn't make contact with the cells that would except such a thing.

Only when I walked in and out of gyms dressed like a businessman did I really feel like my life had purpose! I couldn't quit because I had seen and heard how coach terribly humiliated those quitters!, especially those from Rains he was especially and unthinkably harsh! He called them trifling cowards, and referred to the failures of some of their parents. When I graduated from high school I really needed professional counseling but in those days we were encouraged to be rough and tough. No one wanted be thought of as weak, particularly boys. In my mind I had done everything that I was supposed to do, I was coachable, teachable and obedient. Hard working, and there was no one in the Country that I had seen live or on TV that I thought was better than me all around in all areas than I. Six foot three was the magic number in my State in those days. We had one guy six foot three, the tallest guy on our team and guess who that was, my friend the little light skinned boy had grown up in stature but nothing else, he was still the scariest kid that I've seen until this day. My next door neighbor had been left back and we caught up with him in the twelfth grade, coach simply made a work mule out of him, he was six foot two, and then there was me, only six foot even and I was dunking and playing above and beneath the rim. There was no one on the team who could dunk the ball but myself!

I came to realize that I had learned a valuable lesson from Coach Lefton, never in life again would I ever ever ever give anyone that kind of control over my life again. I was being forced to change my lifelong plans to the effect that no one could ever control my destiny ever again! Coaches have absolutely too much influence over young people and they should be the kind of adult that really follows Jesus.

Only he should lead them in the decisions that they are required to make concerning young people's lives. Coaches have more influence on youth than parents or Pastors of Churches so it is my opinion that they should be very careful in decision making. I have no clue as to the state of mind that coach was in during the time frame that his Oldest son was killed, but I do know that he didn't have any respect for the students from Rains before or after it happened. However I did the right thing, I forgave him completely, but even this day it is difficult for me to relive those years.

May tenth 1966 was one of the happiest days that I had experienced in a long time, it was graduation day. Although I had some very sad memoirs that I would have to change the way that I felt about them, I would have to change my thinking considerably in order to move on. Thanks to my Pastor and my mentor Fess. Fess has a powerful will, he used to be a chain smoker and one day he decided that he would not further damage his lungs with cigarettes anymore and he just quit! Just like that. He did the same thing with drinking about a year later and today I'm happy to say that Fess is a Minister in our community in Rains. He has always been the one that I chose to talk to when I had a problem that I couldn't handle, Fess had the answer.

I had to change my thinking about my Church and my relationship with God as well. Back when I was sixteen years and tried to join our Church, but was denied the privilege because I chose not fake the shouting and showing the symbolic effects of having the Holy Ghost, I felt that somehow the leaders of the Church had separated me from the church and God because they really didn't have the authority to decide who was or was not saved. I always maintained my personal relationship with Jesus Christ through all of my obstacles and disappointments that life threw at me. I had to except the hard fact that you don't get rewarded for working hard and doing the right thing in life always. Keeping your nose to the grind stone does not always work and not for everybody. There were students who were gifted in football and baseball who could not make the transition from those sports to basketball. They were disappointed and walked around campus everyday with nothing to do when Coach cut out all sports programs to make basketball our only sport. Original, would have made an excellent defensive football player.

A step towards freedom

Now that I was out of high school and had the opportunity to leave the nest, I chose to defer my ambiguity concerning going to college. I had enough of school and being told what to do. It was time for me to finally get to see Wall Street in New York City. It was time for me to buy my own car and my own house. I boarded a bus with the friend BB, not my friend but" the" friend BB, Whom neither of us had ever been more than one hundred miles away from home before. We went to Paterson New Jersey and lived with his older sister for about two weeks, just long enough to get our first pay check. It wasn't difficult to find a job as coach had tried to brain wash me even more than he had already done. Jobs were plentiful for seventeen year olds and anyone else who wanted to work.

BB was and is nothing like his older brother who was only one year older than we were, however he was much more matured than us.

It was BB'S brother Billy Jo who actually found us a job and a room to rent. He paid the first two weeks rent and bought food and arranged a ride to work until we could do better. Shortly after we moved into our room BB'S first cousin caught the bus and came to live with us. It was a little crowded but the rent was easier to pay. Everything was going well and suddenly one Sunday afternoon my brother PJ, who lived in New York just drove up as we were just sitting on the stoup and asked me to get my stuff and move to New York and live with him. "New York" I said, how far away is it? Just across the bridge he said, across the bridge, "wow", I ran inside to pack right away. I got all of my things and was off to see the city of my dreams. Crossing the George Washington bridge I began to recall all of the awful feelings that I had endured under a coach, the man that I admired and respected highly.

I remembered being told by my Grandparents and other relatives about how the white slave master would come to the black man's cabin with his young white sons and tell the man of the cabin to stand outside while he and his sons practiced raping the women in the cabin. The man had no power to do anything and neither did the women. I imagined just how terrible it must have been for the women and the husband. Mentally and physically abused and not be able to do a single thing about it, at all. I felt just like that every day and every night, like I was being raped every day and every night and couldn't do anything, and couldn't tell anyone. Everyone knew but didn't dare say anything for fear of having that same thing happen to them. Inferior players were able to get into the games because Arvanie Graves was sitting on the bench getting raped. During practice at recess that I used to enjoy doing my thing had become a terrible burden, a feeling of having one of my hands tied behind my back.

I once heard Roy Wilkins, the civil rights activist say that this feeling was like trying out for the major league baseball team and have the manager say to you just as you are getting up to the plate to hit, "go ahead nigger, you already have two strikes on you but hit a home run, you can do it with the one strike that you have left"! I walked the halls every day and met boys from Rains and other small towns that had seen me play, express disillusion and disappointment. When I walked out on what we called 49, the corner where everyone went to laugh and cut jokes, but everyone got quiet when I showed up. I would just walk away to allow them to continue their fun and not feel saddened for me. Those feelings were too much for a sixteen and seventeen year old boy to bear. There were times of adrenaline rushes in the heat of a game when I seem to almost leap over the top of the backboard. Step into the air at the top of the key and take flight. I'm not hesitant to say that I was unstoppable, no one ever blocked one of my shots since the tenth grade, and that's no joke. If a defender approached me as I was stepping into a jumper, I would move the ball to either side of my head, just brief enough to throw his timing off, and then release the shot with the same follow through, same intensity. I'm disturbed by these feelings so let's get back to the ride across the George Washington Bridge. I saw all of the tall beautiful buildings and bright lights, fascinating. I had no idea that New York was this close to where I was living. I begun to feel my steps towards freedom and I liked it very much. I decided to leave my horrible past on the other side of the bridge, but I found out that it wasn't going to be that easy.

I was glad to be leaving New Jersey; it was a small dirty city with unkept streets, trash cans laying in the street, beer and liquor bottles everywhere. Now! I was even more disappointed at seeing the great New York City! The streets were massively overcrowded with all kinds of people, "Spanish speaking people", Jamaicans, African, Cubans, the Virgin Islands. Every Nationality that you could think of were in New York. Then there were fruit baskets with merchant selling commodities and fruits of all kinds. Fruit that I hadn't seen or tasted before.

The streets were filled with millions of people and cars alike, running on streets that were made from bricks and had no white or yellow lines, cars just rolled down the sides or the middle of the streets. The noise was quiet disturbing to say the least.

The memory of the image that I had from my dreams and imagination suddenly took a great hit, like unto a wind or dust storm but without the dust. I had day dreams of beautiful clean streets with tall shinny buildings. Building adorned with pretty shrubbery, great parks, lakes and streams to look upon. My dreams were greatly diminished, New York had way too many cars and buses, subways and overwhelmed with ambulances and fire trucks day and night, noise.

It was difficult to find the kind of job that I wanted; My brother took me to a manufacturing company that was old and without glamour or integrity, things that didn't interest me. So I did what I had read about, the New York Times had the kinds of advertisements that I was interested in but I would quickly find out that everyone wanted to hire someone with experience, something that I didn't have. But you name it New York had it! I found a job in Manhattan, my first job found on my own.

The job was in a high-rise building overlooking the Hudson bay (river). I was excited but there was no mention of duties, the add only said, no experience necessary, great! Caught my eye right away. I walked into the building and was directed to the janitorial department, although I knew that I was not interested in a janitorial job I would take it and work my way up you know, into an office position ha ha. Well, that idea was a wash, the first assignment that they gave me was to empty all of the trash cans from each desk, desk held by young white girls and white men in the offices. They were all neatly dressed in shirts and ties and the young women wore high heels and lots of makeup.

It was a sea of all white faces and all were trying to be polite by exhibiting the usual fake smile and looking through me as if I wasn't really there! No one spoke to me so I initiated the first Simi-joyful, good morning, silence no one spoke back. It made me feel as if I had mistakenly walked into an all-white restaurant in South Carolina where I had just came from. Surely there must be some mistake, the runaway slaves ran to freedom in the north, this is the north certainly there must be something wrong. I t is a feeling that's hard to describe further with words, it reminded me that I was still a nigger in America, just out of the fields right now. It was the same look that I got when I went down town on Saturdays after working in fields owned by white people. We laughed and played friendly jokes on each other, (the white friends) swam together in the same ponds side by side but when it got right down to it, it really didn't matter if my white friends from their fields saw me on main street, those boys that I could run faster, out swam them in their own ponds which was supposed to make us equal, they didn't know me down town the very next day. I would speak to them, right up in their faces and they didn't see me.

I had been issued a dull colored grey starched and dry cleaners pressed uniform with a mop and bucket. They gave me a large stack of black trash bags to put back into the trash cans after I emptied them. Pretty soon though it was lunch time and I decided that I had had enough, this was no place for a "KING", I decided to take my freedom back, I told the boss to mail my check; Boss was a foreign and forbidden word for me, I would have to become my own boss. My dad was a self employed farmer from the age of eleven when his dad died. My mom was a powerful and smart educated woman who was business minded. Although my dad lost his farm years later, he still walked with that integrity about himself.

I had no intentions of ever seeing that place or the proud white faces ever again. at least until I figure out how to get an office in there. The next day my sister lived in New York also, took me to apply for a job at the hospital that she worked in, Lenox Hill Hospital in down town Manhattan. "Wow" this was a beautiful place to work in and it's located right near the Rockefeller center, great! A well-known TV station and you could see the Stature of Liberty from the top floor of the hospital. Beautiful tall buildings, engineered technology was apparent such that the wind would circulate cool air down onto the street for you on a hot day. This was the New York that I had pictured in my mind, and saw in magazines.

This was more like it; I took a dishwashing job in a huge kitchen, the interviewer told me that mostly college and high school seniors enjoyed working there and that I would have a lot of fun with this job. Everything about this hospital was huge, the union had just gone on strike and won a minimum paycheck for everyone of no less than $100.00 per week, in 1966, fantastic! There were young high school and college kids working and laughing, white, black, Mexican and Puerto Rican, all working together and having fun. This was a place that I could enjoy and learn some things at the same time. The boys were in the dish room and the girls worked on the serving line. There was a swimming pool on the ninth floor and we were allowed to go swimming after we finished the dishes for that particular meal. We were given all of our meals free, and we drank as much juice and fruit punch as we wanted every day. There was a basketball court that we could use on our breaks as well, what more could a young man from South Carolina ask for, young pretty girls too. One day the city boys were bragging about how good they were in sports and the country boys couldn't stand a chance against them, since I was the only boy from the South there, all of the sarcasms were directed at me. They were saying things like, country boys were just country, stuck with a slow paced thought process system in place. (dumb) No country boy could ever hope to be able to compete at anything against the great East coast New York boys.

They arraigned for some of the hot shot playground ballers to meet us on the court after work that afternoon after work. There were about twelve of them altogether and only one Arvanie Graves. Someone made the suggestion that we bet money if I was up for it. They thought that they had a brand new sucker in town but I was no fool. I challenged the big talker that I would bet ten dollars that I would score at least ten points in a game of sixteen points counting by one point each basket, not my team against their team as they suggested. Now, while those city slickers were scrapping up with their knee pads and jerseys that they had stolen from schools and other places, I put my team together on the court and begun to warm up. I didn't look but I heard them snickering and planning the set up to take my money. This is what I asked for, to compete against the best in the world and some were right here. I begun warming up by dunking the ball right off the bat! I put on a display of finger rolls and jump flips from both sides, not exactly a jump hook, the shots were more of a wrist effort from the side at the peak of a leap. Finger rolls both left and right handed, short jumpers, forty foot jumpers, and I threw in some fade away and double pump jumpers. I threw in some left handed jumpers and the like, the bet was already made.

The boys stopped talking and began to ask me if I was perhaps from some other place other than South Carolina? I said no, I'm from a small community called Rains in South Carolina and that there were many with my capabilities there also. I always knew that I was not going to be blessed with height so I compensated that misfortune with skills, unusual skills, I had seen a lot of good players on TV, my feelings for the game transcended good, I had to be great to make it in the big leagues. We proceeded to jump the ball from half court and I got the ball and shot a forty or forty five footer before anyone knew what was happening and it hit net bottom!

And so the game went with me putting on a clinic, scoring eleven of the sixteen points and giving up the ball for the other five baskets to my teammates so that no one could say that I was a ball hawk! It only took one game with me being away from my old high school coach to regain my second most important possession in life to become successful at anything, the first is God given talent that one can developed and perfect, and the second is "confidence". I was gliding through the air and putting my arm almost to my elbow into the rim. Off of the dribble to the left or to the right I would bend my knees in order to get maximum elevation into the air, and at my peak I would hold the shot to get hand, arm, shoulder and body into one unit before releasing the shot, and perfect rhythm. At the last possible second, zoning in on the rim until it looked larger than usual, and then release the shot. I don't know if it made my percentages any better but it certainly made my jump shot contain more form and different from anyone else's.

I was tapping the ball back from offensive rebounds left and right handed and simply befuddling the opponents at every hand. After the game I picked up my fifty dollars and no one ever bragged about any type of sport because I had already beaten everyone at swimming. We won by sixteen to five or six points.

This was the New York that I had imagined, tall colossal looking buildings, clean streets and beautiful stores. I began to notice an older gentleman who lived only a couple of bus stops away from me who worked with us kids in the dish room washing dishing on the first station of the large dish washing machine.

This man came to work every day, the only person older than nineteen years of age in the kitchen. He wore a black suit and tie and carried a briefcase. I found it to be unusual because he also carried a news paper under his arm. The man was ball headed and looked fiftyish but this job didn't require nor was it appropriate to wear a suit to this kind of job. I asked some of the other guys what was up with him, and they thought that the man just wanted to dress like that.

One day as we both sat down together unlacing our shoes and getting ready to change into our white uniforms, I noticed the newspaper that he carried was and old frizzled one and the date on it was for the previous month; Would you believe that this old man couldn't read, he was living in a facade! What was most shocking to me and my ego though was that I surmised that this man must have had the exact same dream that I had as a kid and he didn't make it. He had failed and now he was faking it. When the shift was over the black man would shower, put on his suit and tie and very meticulously take his newspaper, put it under his arm, pick up his briefcase as if he was an executive businessman and walk out into the street as if he had just left his office. I was deeply saddened for that old man and for me also, but God had a different set of plans for my life and I would soon find out what.

When September came I had some very devastating feelings and apprehensions about my life and where it was taking me, or not! The college and high school kids all quit their jobs to return to school and the only ones left in the dish room was guess who? Me and the old black man. Ambiguous thoughts came upon me all of a sudden, at this stage of my life I could either succeed or fail depending on the choices that I made. Fail just like the old man if I didn't call upon some new thoughts about my options. I began to realize that the students who were in my classroom all of my life would not meet this year at school's opening day as usual, and had met like clockwork for the past twelve years.

Those students had become a part of my extended family and now, they had all moved on. I decided to investigate the old man's story whose name was Marvin. I asked, Mr. Marvin, how long have you worked in the dishwasher room? He said thirty years real quickly. "Thirty years", whoa", he said that he had quit school in the fifth grade and there weren't any jobs other than farm work and that only lasted from spring to fall, six months out of the year. He said that his home was in Darlington South Carolina, that's twenty miles from my home town. He said that he had also dreamed of getting his education but winded up getting married because his girlfriend got pregnant, so he got married and ended up with a family of six children instead. He said that he only took the dishwashing job for a few months until he found something better but it never happened. He told me that the best thing that I could do was to go to college right now! And I mean right now!!! I suddenly realized that this old man had flunked out of life and he had just given me some valuable advice because I was headed down that very same road.

I had begun to miss the broken language spoken in my community by the men who got drunk on Friday and Saturdays and hung out on the corner that we called "forty nine". It was a place that I could go and laugh nonstop anytime until it hurt! Some of the men who lived in what we called Crawford Town were the funniest. Timmet would say, Arvanie, how bout keh dish yah pint of ice cream to yo sister Mildred foh me. Now, my sister was a pretty young woman who taught at my high school, and these guys worked digging ditches and such every day. Many times I took the ice cream and ate it on my way home, and never mentioned it to my sister until a month or so later.

The language is so prevalent today until it is like time has stood still in Rains, only faces have changed from fathers to sons and daughters. I remembered the clay hole and the sounds of the old black South that I loved, and I became lonesome for those things. I knew that I wasn't prepared for New York and I really didn't like this city. Those people who had always came back home after living in places like New York, New Jersey Baltimore and Washington DC. and other Large cities were living in a façade and they came home and presented those places as if they were great palaces and wonders of the world. Some were just plain lying about how great city life was. I once saw a man get stabbed repeatedly and died on the street from my fifth floor window, and people just walked by as if nothing happened. The man was continuously screaming, I don't have but two tokens, (worth twenty cents each) and the thief kept stabbing him anyway.

Thinking back about the days that I spent in Paterson New Jersey, My friend's older brother WJ proved to be a natural born leader and had genuine concern for me, unlike the friend BB. In the Bronx where I lived I was trying to decide just how long it would take me to buy my own car and suddenly one day, right out of the blue I received a phone call from mom telling me that my old high school principal had called and said that I should call him right away and I did just that, called principal Noben and he had some wonderful news for me. It seems that the teachers from my senior class advisory committee had selected some students from my graduating class and advised them and also acquired financial aid for them to go to college at various places around the State of South Carolina. About ten students were selected and five of those students went to Morris college in Sumter, about sixty miles from my home. Now, the light skinned boy who used to walk about two miles to my house every morning so that he could ride the bus with me every day so that I would protect him from being beaten up badly by several boys who just didn't like how dirty he was. And partly because of the dirty trick he played on me in the first grade. (you know, right hand lead punch) This boy lived, slept in the same bed, ate with me every morning and every night. We took our first drink of alcohol together. Absolutely not a one of my classmates mentioned anything to me about they were going to college, And BB, never said a word. Not a mumbling word! I wasn't surprised by anything that he did thought, I knew that his character was very suspect every since the first time that I saw him hanging around my cousin and I so that he could gain and steal some fame, he is the same way today. There were six guys out of my senior class who played on the basketball team and we practiced basketball all of recess every day, and we practiced right through the fifth period after recess. That class was taught by a black man, really black man from St. James, another community in our district, I believe he taught us Government or perhaps US history. One day after we all showered and went to class, I just happened to be the last in line to inter the door to his classroom and you wouldn't believe how badly the man yelled at me and told me to get out of his class until I go to the office and get an excuse. My sister Mildred had gotten married and moved away and there was one player on the team who was as dark as I was so the only thing that I could attribute his brutal attack on me was the picture that coach had portrayed me as to the whole school, a "chump".

Anyway, I had friends in the female population in my class and school, allies if you feel me. Tori was a dark female in my class from St Jamse as well and she was the leader of our class, none of the girls did anything without checking in with Tori first, so she stood up and told the Teacher in a matter of fact manner that if he didn't send all of the team players back for an excuse, neither would Arvanie be going for an excuse. She persisted to lambast and jump all over the teacher seriously embarrassing him, and then all of the girls attacked him viciously. I was extremely happy and eternally grateful to Tori for coming to my defense.

Anyway Mr. Noben told me the whole story and he said that he had already made all of the necessary arrangements for my financial aid, and to get me registered for the second semester in January. He also said that he had spoken to the coach and explained the restrained player treatment that I had endured under coach Lefton and that he was certain that I could get a full scholarship the following year with my multiple talent in different sports. He also said that I didn't have much choice or alternatives because the Vietnam War had escalated and I was in danger of being drafted as soon as I turned eighteen in January. The War was too dangerous and big healthy black boys like myself were being sent to the front lines at will;

My mind was made up before I ever hung up the phone, the relationship that I had developed with the principal Mr. Noben, was still bringing me lifesaving assistance from hundreds of miles away. I looked into the heavens and gave thanks to God. I was going to college but before I left New York I was going down town to Wall Street and check out several of the high rise buildings that I would occupy as my office one day, but not in New York.

When Christmas came I was more than ready to go home, leaving behind the city that offered me a learning experience of a lifetime; The next week while I was awaiting time to pass so that I could walk through the next door of opportunity and thought development, Mom and I got a visit from a very prominent white Lawyer who had become rich and famous over the years. He was on the Board of Francis Marion College which was an extension of the University of South Carolina in Columbia, however Francis Marion was just a small college in Florence at the time. Florence is twenty miles away from Rains so I took a ride over to that college and found it to be comprised of four or five buildings. It was just like the Lawyer said, I would be the first black student athlete and one of the first black students attending. The financial opportunities were exceptional like he said but I was no Jackie Robinson so I quickly dismissed the idea of me going to Francis Marion College.

On January 3, 1967 I enrolled at Morris College and on January 10th I turned eighteen years of age on a Monday. I was required by law to report to the local draft board at Fort Jackson in Columbia which was forty miles away. After I was thoroughly examined and as I walked out of the examination ward there were military personnel from all four branches of service running towards me, trying to hustle me into their respective branch of the military, not a chance; I went back to school and that Friday of the same week I received my draft notice, requesting me to report, However the registrar's office had already sent in my deferment form which allowed me to stay in school. I checked and double checked to see if it were possible for me to be excluded from the trip to Vietnam, you see I had two older brothers who had already gone to Germany and one was still there so I knew where I would be going, straight to the "bush".

CHAPTER EIGHT

Interlude with Faith

That Monday morning I found myself walking into the Gymnasium to answer the call to an invitation to try out for the basketball team. There was a posting on the Gym's door for those who had nerve and skills enough to compete. That's what I am so I walked in and was surprised to see three of the players from my high school team and graduating class.

The coach was a huge man, weighting over four hundred pounds and about six foot four inches tall. This coach was from New Jersey and even though I didn't know it right away, there would be yet another lesson to be learned from those who had authority over you. The coach had a line of about twenty try outs standing on the half court line and he was talking to them about "heart", it was a method of demeaning the players that he was going to cut.

I was scraping up on the bench looking on and suddenly I saw coach, starting at the end of the line working his way towards me. He was flipping and dropping a half dollar coin to the floor, over the head of each player such that he would have to turn around to pick it up and while they were bending over to pick the coin up, the one that he chose was unexpectedly kicked as hard as he could in the you know what! Yeh, while the chosen player stooped down to pick up the coin coach put his size fourteen shoe in the seat of each boy's pants and then, directed that kid towards the door! That was the cutting and eliminating process. But who could you tell, there was always the assumption that next year might be better for you.

Coach had been watching all of us play each afternoon after classes into the night, so he had already made his cuts in his mind beforehand." Let the door hit you". I laughed so hard until it was difficult to stop when coach called me over to talk to me. He told me that I would be a good asset to the team but I told him that I needed a couple of days to think it over. He gave me a welcome pat on the shoulder and I started laughing again at my home boys and laughed for the rest of the week. There was a silent code among athletics to keep this kind of abuse to ourselves and away from parents. I was through, I had a great distrust for coaches and authority figures alike, I had taken all of the abuse that I was going to take and decided that God had another way in mind concerning my dream. I had been severely ostracized with mental abuse and now, I've witnessed physical abuse as well. In the days to follow I would receive many invitations to join the team, messages from coach but I declined and avoided seeing coach until I was to tell him about my dilemma in my own way. After the basketball season was over though, and the intermurial sports competitions began, which was what I was waiting for, I formed a team that we called the supersonics, I gave the coaching job to my roommate who weighted about one hundred and twenty pounds. We defeated every team in the competition and then challenged the college basketball team and most of them agreed to play us and we defeated the Morris college team also.

Morris College didn't offer a major in business in those days so I majored in Social Studies which would afford me the opportunity to work in different areas of office and social work as opposed to teaching. I had to take a work study job to help pay my tuition, without the athletic scholarship I needed to supplement my school's funding source. Certainly you wouldn't readily believe the trials and obstacles this job would put me through.

I was assigned to work in the Dean's office and we'll call this guy Dean Martin… He was a short fat black man who was a preacher, and he Pastured a church in Mullins SC. about eight miles away from my home. Dean Martin took me and another guy who was his driver when he went on trips to preach. You see Dean owned several rental properties near and around the college campus, and he showed us how and what he wanted us to do as far as repairs and renovations of different portions of the home only once, and then he would leave us with enough work to last us until late in the middle of the night, almost twelve o'clock each night. The first night Dean came back to pick us up around ten thirty or so and took us over to his house where his wife had prepared a nice dinner and was waiting until Dean came home to eat with us. Fried chicken with all of the fixins. Every night, Monday through Friday we worked until very late at night for hour meals, Dean had absolutely no concern for our studies and homework and there was no one to tell about this treatment. I couldn't very well call home and complain to mom because I thought that Dean was doing us a great favor by feeding me and taking care of my tuition bill entirely since he told me that I didn't need to apply for financial aid. I worked from January until the first week of may just before final exams begun and had been staying up studying late hours into the night. I had no time for myself, or relaxation, I went to class, worked until late, did my studying and back to class again each day. It never occurred to me to check with the Business office about anything I was working for the Dean of the College. Dean had told me but not the other boy, that he didn't need me anymore so, that Monday when I went to pick up my meal ticket I was In for a very serious shock of my life! Dean had been arranging for me to pick up my meal ticket with a phone call up until now without any problems, but now I needed my meal ticket as well as a permission slip indicating that all of my tuition was paid in order to eat and take my final exams. Wouldn't you know that we had finished all of the renovations in all of Dean's properties. The registrar looked over my monthly payment schedule and seemed highly confused so she took it over to her supervisor to check out and then they both came to the window where I was standing, they both asked me with an alarmed look on their faces? Young man, how did you get by all of these months without paying any money at all? I said confidently, I work for Dean Martin Maam, with a proud look on my face; He takes care of all of my bills, they both laughed and looked back at me as if to say, surely you didn't fall for that old trick. I said, you mean that there is no payments made towards my bill" I said well who signed my work study checks. They both stared at each other;

I was appalled, you and dumb, I was confused, they told me that I needed to go and see Dean Martin because Dean was only paying the bills for the other young man who worked with me. They said that there was no indication that Dean had but one student on work study under him and that was his driver, no one was supposed to be working in Dean's personal properties! But in spite of this minor delay as I walked back over to the Dean's office I said to myself, I was working for the Dean of this Great college and I was proud that I had gotten this opportunity to get to know such a powerful man as this on campus.

I knocked on the door of Dean Martin's office as I did every day to go to work in his car. He said come in, I said Dean, there is a minor mistake with my tuition bill in the business office. The little short stubby black man stood up from behind his desk as if he was angry that I had the nerve to come to see him about my bill. He said to me categorically, son, you have to "root little pig or die". Now get out of my office and don't come back! I was floored, this wasn't supposed to happen to me anymore, I was a good kid, I'm in college, my older sister Mildred had successfully completed another college in Orangeburg and obtained the honors of who's who in America. She made the Dean's list constantly, and never had any trouble of any kind. She was teaching school in Germany now, her husband was in the Military. My roommate BB and I were the only ones from my hometown to go to college. BB had managed to get my other little roommate to switch rooms so that he could room with me. Two of the boys who had graduated high school with me had dropped out before the semester ended but the two girls were doing fine. I didn't have a clue as to what to do, it was a Thursday and I didn't have any money to take the bus, I would have to find a way to get home. Going home for any reason would be considered as being a failure.

That night as I layed in my bed thinking and talking to my roommate, he had no money, so he said, and no advice either. This was too much money for me to raise weather it was short notice or not, there was no one in my family that I could ask for five hundred Dollars to take my finals. My whole semester was wasted working for Dean

Martin the crooked Preacher. This man had swindled an eighteen year old kid, a grown man of God, there was no hope. I would have to go back to New York and end up like the old man with the old newspaper and suit and tie, working as a dishwasher for the rest of my life.

It occurred to me that I had known Jesus all of my life, failure and Vietnam was steering me in the face and I could see death at an early age.

How can this be? What did I do to deserve this, having to face the embarrassment of coming home a failure, it wouldn't matter what the circumstances were, who would believe that a well-respected Dean and preacher at a college would do such a thing. In the middle of the night I realized that I had come to college partly to avoid going to Vietnam but now that I was here, I had the feeling that I was supposed to be here, this is where I belonged. There were some very important things that I was supposed to learn from here and not just book learning, this college had taken hold of my spirit and wouldn't let go. I was curious and impressed at the infrastructure and the inner working operations of this school. There was a black president and all department heads were black, there were only black people on the board of directors of this school all the way down to the head chef of the dining hall. Up until now I had no clue as to what type of business that I wanted to go into, It would have to be something like this college. I raised up and got out of bed, I was not going to be beaten again by a black man who had the authority over me. All that I have ever done is think and dream of things that I wanted to happen in my life, things that existed in the invisible and endless world of boundlessness where GOD lives and he sent me to this college, and not only that, he sent me into the world to find some things, things that will propel me into my destiny. It didn't just happen that I've known and developed a special relationship with my Principal Mr. Noben. He didn't just call my mom, know Jesus set me up for this and I'm supposed to trust him to fix this obstacle. So, I told Jesus these words, I can see no hope for me here and I don't know anyone to turn to, where is the door that I'm supposed to go through now? You said that you would always be with me and I certainly need you now, I want to stay in this school. I didn't even call home to tell mom to pray for me for fear that she would worry too much. And I knew that if she told

Dad, Dean would have some trouble! I knew that mom didn't know the inner workings of a college because I didn't know either.

The next morning I awakened refreshed, the worry had gone away so I went to breakfast without the meal ticket and guest what? no one was checking for meal tickets to enter the dining hall. I started looking for a ride home and found one right away, there was a teacher who lived in Marion and I secured a ride with him. I began to tell everyone goodbye and that afternoon as I was just standing around on the steps of the academic building waiting for my ride home, around two o'clock was the time that the teacher from Marion usually left for home. Wouldn't you know, Dean Martin came walking up the steps and said, "what are you two punks doing lounging around out here "by then I had told everyone that I saw weather I knew them or not that Dean Martin had worked me every night until almost twelve, and then he took my work study checks and cashed them and left me hanging, but I will be back. Dean said go someplace else and stand around, my roommate left but there was nothing else that he could do to me so I stayed, and told everyone that I saw just how dirty Dean Martin was and not to let him rip you off as he did me. His authority over me was gone and I was getting angry.

A short while later there was a young, very average looking, nothing particularly noticeable about him, I had never seen this guy before and little did I know at the time that I would never see him again!!! He came up to me on the top step of the academic building and began to make small talk, he acted as if he knew me real well but I was sure that I had never seen him around campus before. He said Graves, What's wrong you seem depressed? I said yes, it seems that I've been working for a crook this whole semester, and now no one seems to be willing to help me even though the people in the business office don't seem to be surprised, as if he has swindled other students before.

Surprisingly this guy knew exactly what I was going through and without hesitation he offered me some very sound advice. He said you must go and see the vice president, Mr. S-------------, he 'll know what to do, he is the acting president and I guarantee you that he can help you. He kept saying his name Mr. S---------------, and then it dawned on me, King Solomon was the wisest king in the Bible, the king that I did the book report on in Bible school when I was a kid. I had always admired this King, not only was he very wise he was compassionate. God had answered his prayer and not only given him the wisdom to rule over his people fairly, he gave him the greatest wealth that the world had ever known for a King. And in my mind I was certainly a king. My Bible said so and I had been crowned King twice already.

I felt the Holy Spirit come over me as it had never done before; I was as sure that Jesus had intervened on my behalf at that moment, and answered my prayers from the night before, I just sat down on the steps, something that I had never done, sat on the steps with my nice trousers on. I didn't even know what the Vice president looked like but I started to walk in the direction of the science building, that's where this plain looking guy told me that he was. Just go over there, anyone will tell you where his office is. As soon as I started to walk over there, there was this handsome young man walking towards me with two other students on each side of him, when one of the girls spoke his name and I heard the familiar sound of my favorite King's name S---------
--------, quite obviously I was extremely happy. Needless to say I was very happy. In addition to the two students on each side of him asking questions, there was also a bunch of other students following behind him. I was extremely happy and content, I had no doubt, I was as sure as I was about knowing that the next day was Saturday as I was about knowing that this guy was the answer to all of my prayers. I proceeded to just walk along for a moment but I quickly decided that my dilemma was definantly much more important than the gibberish that they were wasting this man's time with. So I politely interrupted by saying Mr. Vice President, (you see I don't have permission to use his name) I need to talk to you very badly, he immediately told the girls to go on ahead while I talk to this young man. He ask me if we could walk and talk at the same time, I'm headed over to the business office. Coincidence! I think not. I laid it all out just as it all happened sequentially, just as it all happened. Dean Martin swindled me badly and I could lose this entire semester if I cannot take my final exams. He said Dean should cut out his awful behavior critically effecting these young people's lives and realize that you all are our future. Dean had not only done this kind of

thing to other students before and worst, he had stolen a $250.000 grant check made out to the college and had been threatened by the grantee with jail time if he didn't return it within twenty four hours.

I had no idea that this was a Christian college supported by the Baptist association. I didn't bother to investigate I knew that I could trust Mr. Noben, my high school principal. The Vice president and I walked into the business office and told the personnel person to pull my financial file. Meanwhile I was observing the congenial atmosphere this man generated everywhere he went, everyone in the business office was genuinely happy to see him, laughing and talking to him. He seemed to represent much more than the president's status, he was every body's friend, students and staff alike. He was living his name's sake's reputation of compassion and love. The lady came with my file sadly, Mr. Graves here has not paid one red cent since he's been here. He's been working for Dean Martin though and there's no doubt on that score; Vice President said how much does he owe? Five hundred and thirty dollars. The Vice President didn't hesitate; He took out his check book and wrote a check for the full amount and told the business manager to staple his check to my bill and leave it there until he pays it back, in the meantime give him his meal ticket and exam permission slip to take his exams. The VP didn't have any other business to transact in the business office so he walked out with me. I told him how grateful that I was and that I wouldn't let him down. He said to me as if he had known me all of my life, I know that you will pay the money back, matter of fact like, that's why I agreed to pay the bill for you. He wished me well on my exams and drove away in his car. It was about four o'clock in the afternoon, almost time for the last meal of the day. I was extremely happy, I wouldn't have to try and sneak into the dining hall to eat, and I could chase down my instructors to take my finals that I'd missed. However I wanted to try and find the young man who came to me out of nowhere and advised me to go and see the VP. I wanted to thank him and ask him how he knew that the VP would help me and to find out as much as I could about him. I looked high and low all weekend for that young man, surprisingly his face, there was something about his face, and then there was nothing special about his face, it was troubling, there was absolutely no one on or off campus who knew this guy or anyone who remotely resembled this guy. I was confident In knowing that this fellow had to have been an "angel", and if that's the case I need to remember his face but I couldn't. Just a normal guy apparently but I knew, there was a knowing in my spirit that I couldn't explain.

About ten o'clock that night the thought came to me as if Jesus was speaking to my mind and I was hearing him in my ear. My roommate was asleep and everything was quiet. I heard loudly in my ear, Arvanie, I'm with you, even to the ends of the Earth. I realized that God had sent an angel to direct my steps that day and that I would never lay eyes on that young man ever again. I was in awe, I knew for the first time in my life that I was on the right track that God had created for me before I was ever born. I was in the right place at the right time and there would be other obstacles to come into my life to test my faith and I shall trust in the Lord my God always. God had sent me a personal message by his messenger and he made sure that I knew it. I knew that my destiny was through the doors of this College and it didn't matter how I came to be here, God was with me and I had no doubts of his presence all around me. What I didn't know was that one day in the future I would be communicating this same kind of faith to some of God's people, those who have ears to hear me. When I heard the name of my favorite King, there was no better way of convincing me of the message. The only person place or thing that I think of more than God is "Solomon", God said that we should love him with "all our heart" all our "strength" all our "Soul" and all of our "mind". My thinking would be given all control unto God. I gave him control of my mind so that I could control the thoughts that I would allow to linger and expand. When I found myself carelessly day dreaming and thinking the same thoughts every day, I would circle that thought in my mind and move it away, little by little until I replaced it with new thoughts that seemed impossible. It seemed impossible for me to found and build a college alone. But I had determined that each human was sent into the world to solve a problem. I had found my problem and I would think of ways to solve it before hand. I found that there were absolutely no institutions of higher learning that would teach black people the process of building and managing their own businesses. Only colleges that offered degrees in business administration, business management etc. How to gain a position as CEO'S in other folks companies that they had built. I began to think of my past that God would use as an obstacle for me to overcome and develop my faith.

COMMUNICATING WITH FAITH

At the age of sixteen, the Sunday that I was led by the Holy Spirit to go forth and join the house of the Lord, my home Church. It never occurred to me that anyone would deny me the opportunity to join my father's house, it blew me away! Who would refuse a child the right to join his own home Church? Particularly one that my Grandfather hope to build with his own hands, one that I had worked and taught Sunday school in most of my life. That act caused me to believe that somehow the people of this Church had separated me from God, but now my beliefs had been vindicated by the messenger. From that day forward I begun to go to the library to seek wisdom from the wisest men and greatest minds the world has ever known. Men like Ptolemy, Diocletion Pythagoras the Greek who believed in Metempsychosis, the eternal reoccurrence of things, and the mystical significant of numbers. Deucalion, Ptongeles, Einstein, Socrates and most of all, King Solomon!

In a book called (Solomon and Sheba) I found that historically, from the Bible's perspective there had been a long line of Queen Candace's in Ethiopia. The Queen of Sheba brought along with her as gifts, Gold and animals, silk and dye for coloring, she also brought along eleven young maidens who were virgins for the King's pleasure after she would leave to go back to Ethiopia. Theoretically they were all of a beautiful caramel colored complexion as most Ethiopians and same as the Queen. Their heads had all been shaved completely bald and they had all been dressed in sack lack garments from head to toe! The Queen had taken the Liberty to try and confuse the wise King Solomon deliberately, to prove that she was wiser, and disprove all tales that she had heard for many years. She had inserted four males dressed exactly as the females, eleven females, all eleven years old. None had developed breast yet, and no makeup, they all looked identical. This would be one of many tricks that she would use to try and confuse the King, this one being her surprise winner she thought. When she asked the King to look them over carefully and try to identify any difference in any of them if he could. The King took his time, something that took me a long time to develop, patience;

The wise King summoned his servants to go and bring him eleven pieces of fruit, and to place one piece directly behind each individual; The Queen praised him for gaining the love of all of his servants and slaves as well. They were all wearing gold necklaces and bracelets with matching clothing, slaves and servants alike. After the servants placed the pieces of fruit behind each of the eleven maidens the King told them one by one to turn around and pick up the fruit. The King Solomon was looking for mannerisms and agilities of each person. As the King noticed he called out and separated the maidens who stooped down holding both knees together completing the task easily. There were four out of the group though who leaned over, allowing one leg and foot to extend out backwards, these he determined to be boys. The Queen looked at him in total surprise and told him that the half had never been told about his wisdom. In one thousand years no one had been able to determine any difference in the trick of the maidens. The boys were awkward and aimlessly bending over to pick up the fruit. It was one of the many tricks that she had planned for the King but he answered them all with ease and very little effort on his thinking. I realized that thinking was indeed a very powerful tool and I would have to change my mind about many things in the years to come.

COMMUNICATING WITH WISDOM

While I was in college my name went through some variations, changes to accentuate my personality. A name is one of the most important things In a person's life, it represents your character and the way that people think about you upon first impressions. I was highly sensitive about my name

Edward Alvanie Graves, too many parents named their sons Edward in the black communities for the like of intuition and awareness of other names for their sons that would set them apart as someone special, or a son whom they dreamed would do great things. African names

Ed Graves

were out because we only knew derogatory and degrading things about Africa. Edward, the name of a British king captured the attention of many parents who wanted to present their sons in that light, but the problem that I had with the name King Edward, was involved greatly in the massive slave trade and besides, too many wimps were named Edward, to exclude myself of course. So to help out the practices of our heavy tongued Southern black people I dropped the L in Alvanie and changed it to Arvanie. The students at Morris thought that I was mispronouncing my own name simply because they had never heard of the name before. My father named me after his Grandmother who was named Arotii with connections to Africa. Later in life after interring the business world and having to pronounce my name hundreds of times per day I simply couldn't take the butchering of Arvanie Graves so I changed it to ED GRAVES, which has stayed with me every since. Except in my home town where everyone can say Arvanie so beautifully, makes me very happy to go home to visit. There were so many absurd attitudes and pronunciations of my name until it was not even funny in the least, made me want to fight sometimes! (just kidding).

This brings me back to the nights that I sat on the bench on our basketball team in high school. I had begun to develop my mind so that I could change my dilemma at will and avoid the sadness that I felt by traveling in my mind to New York and becoming a business tycoon. I often wished that there was some way that I could arrange to be kicked off of the team because I could not quit! I could never have lived with the idea that I couldn't cut it so I quit, never happened.

Sitting on the bench was like being a slave and forced to do ditch digging work while I watched the white people with less skills working as master masons and architects, building designers etc. and knowing in my heart that I was a architect from long ago. When I prayed to Jesus and asked him to help me with my tuition at Morris the communicating with faith factor came in when I surrendered all to him. I just gave up completely, there was nothing that I could do and there was no hope without him. I didn't allow any doubt to enter my mind. The Japanese masters say, when the student is ready, the teacher will appear! Jesus had solved my problem with human involvement and it would be humans who helped me to reach my destiny. It was time for me to consult the mind of the greatest thinker of all times—"KING SOLOMON".

Understanding that God's spirit is everywhere at all times, it always has been and always will be. Spirits never die, "Satan is a spirit" and can never die so why waste time talking, thinking and worrying about him, God will handle him. God finished my life at its end and then went back into the womb and started my beginning. I know that he has placed gifts and talents in my spirit before I was ever born and he made the connection in the womb. I know that if I recognize and acknowledge my gifts and talents and patiently and diligently perfect them, God will send the other help that I need to complete my destiny. I've chosen not to worry anymore about the people that come into my life to hinder me, but I do look for those tendencies in people and I avoid them as soon as possible. So I said to myself, I'm ready to become a successful businessman in the invisible world of spirit, I'm not absolutely sure which business, but I'm leaning towards a business college, and now all that I have to do is believe it without a doubt and apply my gifts.

Solomon said to me in Proverbs, a book that he wrote, verse seven, "fear of the Lord is the beginning of knowledge" but fools despise wisdom and instruction; So then, if I revere the Lord and seek his guidance, he will lead me to my destiny and purpose in life. A fruit tree has no use or need for the fruit that it bears, it bears fruit for mankind to enjoy. If a grape is not picked when it is fully ripened, nature will force it off of the vine.

But who can say that the grape has lived its life in vain if it falls to the ground uneaten. The juices from the grape seeps back into the ground and ends up right back into the root again to start the cycle all over again. It is then recycled rechanneled back through the vine again and hence, the re-occurrence of things and life everlasting!

I've come to realize that the people that we come in contact with throughout life, each have a special lesson to teach us, and the more painful the lesson, the more important it is to accomplishing our goals. My coach taught me unknowingly to never allow anyone to influence my thinking negatively, and never let anyone determine the path to my destiny. Some people should be avoided and some should be followed for a time.

In a book called "Solomon and Sheba", written by Dr. James B. Prichard, the Ethiopian version reveals that it took over six months by caravan for the Queen of Sheba to reach Jerusalem, which was about fourteen hundred miles distance between Jerusalem and Ethiopia! Solomon had been informed by his many spies that she was of a (Jeni) tradition and possessed magical powers. She was also said to have been born with a club foot. (animal's hoof-foot). The story goes on to suggest that Solomon engaged in some strategic planning to prepare for her visit! He ordered his best master builders and masons to construct in his genuinely large parlor beginning at the entrance way, Three extravagant golden steps. Then, the digging of a large pool to enclose half of the entire parlor! The pool was about two feet deep and inlayed with clear glass at the bottom. He placed beautiful and exotic fish with magnificent colors of "bright orange, red, gold and purple" throughout the enclosure! Exotic gems, Rhine stones, diamonds and rubies adorned the walls and furniture. Large gold chains hung around the walls and on great ivory pillars. Solomon's entire palace was breathtaking! At the entrance gate into the City of Jerusalem Solomon had arraigned a welcoming parade and procession of two thousand of his most extravagant chariots, horsemen and Arabian Stallions to lead her to his palace. His entire objective was to get a glance at her feet as soon as she walked in and lift her garments to step into the pool which was between the entrance of his palace and his Royal chair. He wanted to know exactly what he was dealing with, pure woman or witch before introductions were made! Weather she was of a demon orientation or normal woman without a club foot. When the Queen reached the palace, Solomon did not go out to greet her, he had his maidens escort her in. There were two massive golden lions positioned on either side of the entrance way. As soon as she saw the King seated on his throne in his beautiful purple robe with golden sashes around his waist, hanging down to his feet, beautiful birds of all kinds seated in uniformed obedience, she immediately realized that Solomon could communicate, not only with the birds but the exotic fish in the pool also. Things that she had been told by travelers who perked her curiosity years ago. She knew that he was endowed with great wisdom, wisdom of which she had never known. She had heard of Guru's who had the powers of mental telepathy but now she was witnessing it being displayed first hand by the King.

King Solomon commanded two of the larger fish to leap out of the water in front of the Queen and greet the Queen by lying down still, and then make their way back into the water. He commanded two of the beautiful birds to fly over and take hold of the Queen's see through gauze like garments on each side, and lift it up enough for him to see both feet were normal, and then flew back to their respective places. The Queen was so amazed and excited that she lifted up her Simi see through clothing and stepped into the pool in great laughter! Another occasion that she said, the half has never been told, two of many over the next three days. And so did all of her unsuccessful tricks go. She fell into his arms and around nine months later, "Meneleke" their son was born in Ethiopia.

BILL CLINTON-"Weed", not inhale? Why not?

Even though I didn't get the opportunity to formally give my life to Christ in my home Church by confessing before men with my mouth, and saying that Jesus Christ is Lord, he died and arose on the third day, I had developed my own relationship with Jesus. It was always my intention to experience alcohol and drinking as the men before me had done for centuries; It seemed like a young man's tradition and right of passage into manhood to experience such things. We made it a point to get together after classes on Fridays and have a party at Morris. However there was this one occasion where my roommate and I stayed on campus this particular weekend and as we were on our way to the liquor store, which was on the corner, as we called it, (there's a corner in every neighborhood), near the campus. An upper classman approached us, he was from the Pee Dee area also, same as us. This guy sold weed and we didn't know anything about weed. Actually weed wasn't openly talked about around campus in those days. But somehow he managed to talk us into trying it, even though we were both afraid of it, we couldn't let on that we were. Well, this boy convinced us to try one joint that cost me my last five dollars and my roommate 's too, money that I won playing tunk gambling, dumb, dumb, and dumb!

We didn't even know how to smoke it, we smoked Winston's. So, he showed us how to inhale and "hold it" by smoking most if it himself.

He said to me, take a puff and hold it in your lungs until it burns, and then blow it out! We will call him, LG. He said that it would be cheaper than liquor in the long run and there's no hangover, and it wouldn't take as much to get high as liquor. This guy was a good hustler and we were dumb and dumber.

The very first puff that I took burned my throat tremendously and LG was standing right there coaching, hold it a little longer, little longer! The weed aggravated my throat and lungs. Now, I was highly aware of the dangers of the asthma that I had as a child and here I was, in College, smoking weed, asking for the same trouble all over again. This stuff was nothing like smoking cigarettes; It was downright painful to me. As both my roommate and I started coughing LG kept urging us to take another puff, one puff is not enough!

My roommate and I BB, both looked at each other as we usually did when we occasionally wanted to run a Conn, and we decided that this wasn't for us. It would not be cool though to turn it down or refuse to finish the one joint after we had paid for it and started smoking it. We couldn't show fear that's really not cool, so when he passed it back to me I faked it, as well as BB. I pretended to inhale when I wasn't even taking in any smoke at all. We couldn't let on that we were afraid of the weed but that's exactly how it went down. Bill Clinton didn't lie but the media is not the place to fess up if you don't intend to be made a fool of! We faked the inhale and passed it on until it was gone. The guys that smoked it regularly and loved it couldn't understand why we never wanted to smoke it again because they thought that everyone should love it as they did.

Pot was suppose to be so good and make you think better was a lie for me. It did make me really hungry and apprehensive, scared. I didn't like it then and I never ever put myself in that situation ever again until this day. If it is good to you and you like it, you keep it to yourself! I'm still angry at myself for being so gullible, and that night I wanted my money back so that I could buy the liquor that I wanted in the first place. When the semester ended and I passed all of my exams as usual, I headed back to New York for the summer.

I got my old job back washing dishes which I really enjoyed. It was a college boy's dream, I ate all of my meals for free and they were good, unlike the meals that you get when you're sick. I enjoyed immensely the use of the swimming pool where I could further develop my swimming skills.

I had been dating a beautiful young lady from Mullins, near my home town who was a few years older than I was and it seemed to be a very prudent thing for me since I was intent on dating several girls at the same time anyway. I didn't want to make the mistake of getting her pregnant because I had learned all of the bad things not to do from my dad and many other men, if I wanted to be a good dad and that's just what I had my mind and heart sat on. I knew that I was a good man and I wanted all of my children under the same roof with me when the time came for me to get married.

I arrived in New York and just as I had gotten settled and started back to work on my old job, you guessed it, I received a call from my girlfriend, she was in New York too! It happens that she had family living in N.y. also. Now when it came down to our sexual intimacies she told me that there was no need for me to use any protection, she said that she was on the pill. Wow, I felt safe and happy. We had talked about safe sex and even though I didn't like condoms I was just going to live with the idea, no children out of wedlock for me. I thought that it would be really nice to have my girlfriend from home spend the summer with me, she was such a beautiful girl and I didn't have to use protection, Whoa! You don't have to guess that this would prove to be a big mistake indeed!

Three weeks after she arrived in New York she told me that she was pregnant, and not only that, she said that I would have to forget about going back to college in the fall, I should just move in with her. Whoa, wait a minute now! She went on to say that we would have to settle down and raise a family, in a city that I didn't like other than the summer job and visits. Here It was starring me square in the face all over again, the old man in the dish room wearing a suit to work every day to impress my neighbors. What a bummer, she was twenty five and I was only eighteen, way too young for me to get married, after all of the trouble that I had with Dean Martin, trying to stay in school, and then there's the Vietnam War, I had to find a way to get back to Morris College.

I was afraid, I was sad, how was I going to tell mom after all of the plans that we had made, I was trapped and knew it.

School was the right place for me to be, I had taken several steps towards my destiny threw the doors of Morris College. I told (Pat) that I would have to go home and talk to mom and her mom as well. I liked and respected her mom greatly so I went back to South Carolina at summers end. I girded up my loins, my nerve and went to have a sit down talk with my girlfriend and her mom one afternoon on the couch that I liked. I told Pat's mom just how dangerous it would be for me to drop out of school with the fighting fiercely hot in Vietnam. The only thing that was keeping me out of the war thus far was the fact that my college was required to send in the deferment form for students who maintained academically above a -c- average. I asked her to help us until I finished college and I would do the right thing. I could take better care of my child with a college Degree. She understood perfectly and allowed me to go back to school. I chose to be a man and not run away from my responsibilities.

CHAPTER NINE

Equating Wisdom to having fun

Back in high school I remember my mentor Fess, once told me that in order to get over the pain and dis-comfort of falling in love with someone who could unfortunately not, or was not simply meant to be, and would never materialize into a lasting relationship, If you dated several girls at the same time, not only would the effects of love diminish, the possibility of falling in love again would be difficult. The protected level of emotional presence focused on several women as opposed to dating and concentrating all of your heart and emotions on one girl. If you felt your heart connecting more to one than the others, it was time to break that relationship off. Pretty selfish but it works.

It would have been too dangerous for a King such as Solomon to continuously focus all of his attention on one love as he did for a while with the Queen of Sheba. But during the second half of the 955 to 960 BC era Queen Hatshepsut ruled the neighboring and world powerful Egypt, (Egypt is the name of black HAM'S OLDEST SON). However the dangers of a King falling in love with one woman is reflected in the charismatic female leader of Israel, Deborah. Furthermore within both Egypt and Israel, Queens shared in the influential affairs of leadership with their King husbands. There has only been documentation of the Queen's birth and reign, Sheba, the land of Canaan, which is the old name for Ethiopia, and also the name of one of Ham's sons who were listed in this order, CUSH, EGYPT, PUT AND CANAAN! (Solomon and Sheba) a book written by Dr. James B Prichard, and (the Black Presence in the Bible) by Rev. Walter A. McCray.

In my case the process of selecting a wife would require a calm objective selective approach with a wide range of experienced attributes and behavior patterns of a woman. Her health and also her families overall health history would have to be considered. Most of all she would have to be compatible and complementary to me with beautiful legs!

The first girl that I ever dated at age fourteen had some very beautiful legs, she was from ST. Mary SC. After considering all of the attributes of a wife that I was interested in I quickly realized that I had absolutely no idea where to start looking for a wife, so I just dated until I got ready to give up on my wisdom and I asked God to send the wife to me.

While at Morris I had the very sad occasion to watch and witness the exact same thing that happen to me during my bleak basketball career. There were two exceptional ball players, one of which was attending the University of South Carolina and the first black player to enter their athletic program, and the other was a brother from Conway SC. that we called Diamond. The USC guy was from Dillon sc., about twenty miles from my home town. During basketball season for two or three years running, this guy was scoring forty plus points per game but when he entered the ranks at USC he sat on the bench just like I did, watching inferior players run the court every night. My senior year was approaching and one evening I was reminiscing, reshuffling the events of my past and categorizing the good verses the bad things that happened in my life. I was checking out the Bible categorization of the seven years of lean and seven years of plenty.

Realizing that the normal vicissitudes of life will simply occur from time to time. Unfair occurrences will prevail seemingly for a while, but if you keep on pushing you will overcome and good will be yours in the end.

Thinking back to the first summer after my first semester at Morris College, after being swindled by the Dean of the school, working for five months for him in his rental properties, and then he kept my work study checks for himself. I realized that with God's help I had overcome an overwhelming adversary with great power. And then three weeks later I was swindled by my girlfriend with the pregnancy deal. The birth of my child that I would not be able to raise under my own roof. The day after she told me, my brother in law took us to Coney Island, a huge recreation park in NY. The place was packed on this bright summer day and as soon as we walked in through the entrance, amazingly after only about ten feet inside the park, a young boy came running up to me and grabbed my arm and told me that his mother wanted to see me right away! He pointed to a trinket and toy stand where there was this foreign looking Egyptian middle aged lady waving fiercely with great excitement to get my attention to come over. I told the boy that I didn't know her and that I didn't believe in fortune tellers. He proceeded to tell me that she wasn't into fortune telling for money, she was gifted, I said what does that mean gifted? Suddenly the woman started walking towards me and yelling out loud, hey, "you with the woman with the bastard child". Now that got my attention, I was angry and embarrassed at the same time.

I had just found out yesterday that my girl was pregnant and I had never been to Coney Island before in my life, had never seen this woman before and she knew that my girl was carrying my child who was about the size of grape seed. No visual appearance of pregnancy. So I walked over to her stand and she sat down and told me that as soon as I walked through the gates she could see the shinny, glowing presence all around me and it was the Holy Spirit. The Spirit told her to tell me that I would do some great and wonderful works for the Lord in my later years. And that I would be teaching and Preaching for the Lord, and the child that my girl was carrying would be blessed also. There would be many trials to overcome but don't worry, in your later years the Holy Spirit would direct my path. Now all that I needed to do was to go back home, tell someone in my family just what she said, and you better believe that someone would certainly try to push me into the pulpit the very next day. I wasn't interested, all that I wanted to do was drink liquor on Fridays and date as many pretty girls as I could. Preaching did not fit into my business plans, preachers don't make any money!

REMINISCING

During the summer of 1970 I realized that I had just completed the best learning experiences of my college career. I had been assigned a work study job in the campus book store and the store manager allowed me to read all of the books that I wanted to, to include taking the books to my room to read and ponder over. I also took out a subscription to US News and world report for my current events study. I attended summer school the previous summer and my eyes were opened to some wonderful and enlightening ideas. I took black history that summer for the first time in my life and the course was taught by a young black man who was the President's younger brother. We called him "Earl the pearl" because of his (swazaa), suave appearance. Earl was the best looking black man that I had ever seen! He had black wavy hair and a long black mustache with the ends on each side curled upward towards the sky. He dressed immaculately with his shinny shoes, matching pants, necktie with a contrast in his jacket or suit, everything matched. He introduced himself as a young man who had never seen the inside of the eleventh or twelfth grade classrooms but he held two masters degrees. Immediately following that statement he said, now class, let's bring the slaves out of "Africa". I was truly inspired, I had come to a college that was totally owned and operated by black people, there were no whites on the board of directors but there were some white, Indian and French instructors on board. I never dreamed that it was God's plan for me to be the founder and owner of my own Bible Business college. I was dreaming of owning a business structured just like this college was, with black heads of departments and divisions etc.

Earl opened my eyes to a different kind of Africa than the one that I was accustomed to seeing and hearing about. He taught us about an Africa that we could be proud of, moreover the progress that the country was making was astonishing. My uncle who had been to Africa in the military in the forties and early fifties, would come to our school and show film of a people living in a degraded scope of existence. Those film were depressing to me because I had adopted a different perspective of Africa and Earl was teaching the histories of a people who had been the first to develop the study of mathematics and medicine. A totally different ideology of where I was descended from. So it came to pass that I would read everything that was in the bookstore pertaining to my heritage historically about Africans and African Americans.

I went back to New York during the summers until finally I received my final draft notice and it informed me that there would be no need for me to register for my final fall semester at Morris because I would be inducted into the armed forces that October. The last week before I was to leave New York I went to the bank and drew out all of my summer savings, around three hundred and fifty dollars, only to have my pocket "picked clean" in broad daylight. One moment I was walking with the cash in my wallet down on 125TH street to pick up a suit that I had on layaway and the next minute my wallet was gone!

The most horrific and devastating feeling in my life, I couldn't believe it! I had a feeling of abandonment by Jesus, a feeling of sadness and loneliness all at the same time, the feeling held me motionless for about fifteen minutes just looking around for some kind of joke or clue. Finally a sudden calmness came over me and brought me back to the reality of where I was, and what I would have to do next. There were way too many obstacles appearing out of nowhere with the intent and purpose on keeping me out of Morris College. I went to my supervisor on my job and asked if I could stay on and work another two weeks and she said yes.

I had decided that if I was going to go to war in Vietnam Nam anyway and probably get killed or maimed, I was going to live a little in Baltimore where my older brothers from the other side of my family lived. I caught a bus and went to Baltimore, I got a job right away working at a smeltering company. I met some young men working there who had just recently gotten out of the armed forces and they told me in no uncertain terms that Vietnam Nam was no place to be and that it was a good thing that I hadn't received my draft notice yet! One of the young men told me something that was quiet liberating and informative. He had just gotten out of the Navy and he said that if I were to go down to the Navy recruitment office on Baltimore St. and volunteer the draft, that I could not be drafted under any circumstances because he had done that very thing, serving his tour of duty in the Navy.

The analogy behind this idea was that the Navy doesn't draft anyone and I would have the opportunity to travel in the service without being on the ground where all of the intense fighting was taking place. I eagerly took his advice and sure enough one Friday evening after work I went down and talked to the Navy recruiter, he told me that I should take the entrance exam and in the meantime he would send for my draft notice papers from my local board in Marion SC. I took the exam and scored in the upper highest percentile and that I was already scheduled for nuclear training in England, "whoa", that's way across the pond isn't it? I loved the idea though, as long as I didn't have to risk getting killed or disturbed mentally or maimed it was fine with me! A couple of weeks later I received a call from the Navy Recruiter and he gave me the good news, he said that he had my draft papers transferred to Baltimore and that I didn't have to worry anymore, I could not be drafted! He said that I had plenty of time, there would be no rush for me to come down and take the oath of induction. Go and have some fun with the American girls before I left. That same Friday night I went out to celebrate and have some fun indeed! I found myself sitting in a bar at a table alone because it was early and things hadn't started jumping yet! I was waiting for my brothers to get off work so that I could tell them the good news. While sitting there sipping on a glass of cutty sark scotch and ginger ale I noticed that those liberating words kept coming back into me head "you cannot be drafted now". All young men regardless to where they were in the late sixties and seventies, there was a fearful feeling always with you. War! And there's absolutely nothing that we could do about it. Now I could not and would not be drafted, I was directed to take matters into my own hands and it was truly liberating. Suddenly it clicked, the Navy doesn't draft anyone either, why should I go down and take the oath ever?

At that moment I decided to go back to Morris College and finish what I had started, I'll get the extracurricular wisdom that I was seeking! I stayed in Baltimore and turned twenty one years of age on January 10, 1970 and it was on. I could legally go into any club or bar and party, party, party! At the end of the summer I went back to Morris and begun to read tirelessly to learn as much as I could about what the wisest men who ever lived had to say about God, and all of his creations. I chased Diogenes, Diocletian, Patanjili, but most of all I chased Solomon! I also wanted to observe everything that I could about the infrastructure of operating a college. Returning to the unpredictable concepts of the mind concerning justice, love, trust and loyalty, many things seemed to be uncertain. I surmised that it was time to contact my father in Heaven.

MY PRAYER

I decided to ask God for the things that I needed to usher me into my purpose and calling in life, very similar to the "Jabez Prayer", but I didn't stop there I asked for the desires of my heart also.(my dream).

Dear Lord, in the mighty name of our savior, Jesus Christ. For my personal happiness please grant me the wisdom to become the owner of a 1972 Cutlass Supreme Oldsmobile (it was the fall of 1972), I want a nice office job in a congenial work atmosphere. A nice home in Columbia, and Lord most of all I want you to select my wife because I have absolutely no idea how to begin to look for such a thing! Now unlike Adam, I will describe my wife to you. She must have "beautiful legs" first of all, and one who is compatible with me, be of a medium brown complexion and I want to be married by the time I'm twenty five years old. I want two children about four years apart to prevent having them both in college at the same time. I want my children to be out of school by the time I reach fifty years of age so that my wife and I can travel through Egypt and Africa at large.

After laying it on the line to God with my petitions, I went on with my life without ever thinking about the matter ever again, I left it all in the hands of the Lord. It seems kind of silly now but back then I had since enough to know that nothing of any significant happens without GOD. Yet later in life I thought that I could became a successful businessman on my own simply because I was gifted under my own power.

The next spring as prom season was approaching I had dated several girls but I wasn't particularly interested in taking anyone special.

PRAYER ANSWERED

And then there was this beautiful spring morning, I was between classes and just standing around with some other fella's on the back steps of the academic building, just kicking it you know. It was the rear entrance of the building facing the girls dorms and dining hall, as we did almost every day. However this would turn out to be a very special morning, a morning that God had chosen to introduce me to my future wife!

There was the sweet smell of spring in the air and the trees had clothes themselves with beautiful blossoms and thick and rich green leaves. The young ladies were dressing for cooler climates and "hot pants" were in style. When they walked by you could smell beautiful fragrances of perfumes and hair care products. I was kidding around with some of the guys about the girls who had the prettiest legs and as they walked by, we turned around to get a passing look! Well, suddenly and miraculously, I seemingly had an optical illusion! I noticed that the Sun was peeking through the leaves of the trees where the branches were almost parallel with my view towards the West at about 9:50 am, it was bright! I was standing on the top step looking through the leaves visualizing a sparkling dancing of the Sunlight, I noticed three young girls walking towards us laughing and talking on their way to class. What I had my vision locked in on though, was the girl in the middle, she was wearing a caramel colored slipover short sleeve sweater, with the exact same matching colored shorts. Well, the girl's skin color was the same color as her clothing and I couldn't tell if she was wearing any clothing at all or not! As I said previously, "hot pants" were in. The girl's outfit was matching her skin color perfectly and the sunlight was reflecting a cohesive blend. For a moment I thought that I might have been still buzzing from having a few drinks the night before, but I hadn't had anything to drink at all. I knew that something had to be wrong with my picture though because no one else said anything, or even noticed the girl, I was hesitant to speak so I waited until they got closer and I saw that it was indeed just the outfit!

When this young lady came up the steps my eyes were glued on her, she weighted about one hundred and ten pounds with a cute face, but most of all she had perfectly shaped beautiful legs, front and back! As she passed by me my right hand just went on its own and patted that young lady on her behind before I knew it! "Ka-paaw" out loud I said with my eyes closed expecting her to put five fingers right up on my jaw! Something that I would normally never do, That's something that would get you thrown out of school, quickly, no questions asked! immediately following the incident though, my mind and faculties returned to me as my eyes were still closed, I felt the young lady reach up and kissed me on my cheek, I said "ca-pai-yaw" as if she had slapped me. This girl had kissed me gently and softly on my cheek and I didn't even know who she was? So I followed her into the building. I said hey, what's your name and why did I get the kiss? She replied, I know you though just like everyone else on campus knows you, you're ED Graves everyone knows you; I said, would you like to go to the prom with me? She said yes but only if you quit all of your other girlfriends. I said what other girl friends? She said don't even try it, every girl on campus knows you and they're waiting to see who you take to the prom. I said OK it's a date.

Her name was "Celia Durant" from Greenville SC. we went to the prom and had a marvelous evening, little did know that she would one day be my wife.

When I went to my dorm that evening and as I was laying on my bed that night thinking, I asked my roommate if he knew anything about her and he said yes, I know her she's in one of my classes, she's a nice girl from Greenville. But there was something different about this girl and it was bugging me terribly, like no other girl had ever done. For one thing she had waay too much nerve, who was she to give me, Arvanie Graves an ultimatum, asking me to quit other girls that I was dating, and stood her ground as if I could take it or leave it!

She was not afraid of missing an opportunity to date ED Graves, a 205LB six foot tall good looking cat. When I told the numerous girls who had asked me to take them to the prom that I was taking Celia, they all got angry with me, but mad with Celia.

As weeks went by and we got to know each other better she told me that everyone knew me, they had seen me play ball and they knew that coach had been trying to get me to play for the school team but

I refused. There would be days to come when many of the girls on campus wanted to fight Celia so I advised her to move out of the dorm off campus, she was a year behind me and the next year she moved off campus after I graduated.

CHAPTER TEN

Young Free and Black in America

During our lifetimes we all have encounters with coaches, advisers, leaders and others who shed influences in different areas of our lives. I remember when Jim Brown, ex-pro football player said in an interview that once he went to the Cleveland Browns, the coach told him these words,--Jimmy, we're going to build our entire offence around you! You're going to be our go to guy. That was all that it took to place the great Jim Brown into his own element. He had the complete trust and confidence of his coach, moreover the team just happened to carry his last name, "the Browns"!

A good coach is expected and required to extract a player's best potential from promising players, not to confuse or certainly not degrade an athlete in front of his teammates and peers. Particularly when a coach has single out and targeted a player to break his or her will and destroy his confidence. How is it that a player is to be punished for doing everything good and right young players who have not even discovered their own strengths and full potential. There will always be coaches for helping you make important decisions throughout life, as a wise writer wrote, "when the student is ready, the teacher will appear".

Someone will influence you as to which Church you should go to, what schools to attend, which career jobs to except or apply for etc. These options are all under the suggestion of mind control either by you or someone else. It is written in the our fathers prayer, thy kingdom come thy will be done on earth just as it is in Heaven, those who have ears, let them hear.

When we read the Bible story of Esau and Jacob, the two twins who were born to represent two Nations of people. From the very onset in the mother's womb, Jacob, the younger twin grabbed whole of the older brother Esau's foot and tried to pull him back so that he could be born first. Those boys already had a since of their destiny and purpose in life. God was not directing the steps of Jacob in this act, which illustrates the ideology that we all come from the invisible world of spirit with choices which indeed is a world of endlessness and boundlessness, even before conception! Therefore when we are born we're not only made in the physical but spiritual likeness of God as well, having the creative spirit to create physical things out of the nothingness of that invisible world of spirit. We are in this world but not of it. This simply means that the spirit of God lives within us from birth throughout life and the world of spirit is where it will return at the end of life to be judged by God.

When our physical assignment on earth is completed or neglected, having been sought after, we will return to God's Kingdom which is all around us, invisible. Having faith within our minds and heart is the most powerful spirit of existence on earth and in heaven. Once you come to realize that before each human being is born, God places a part of his spirit within us, and in that spirit he establishes a dream in our hearts. Symbolic of a tree which has many branches, each with its own gift or talent which we must develop and cultivate into its fullest potential on earth. Once you have found your calling and assignment, discovered your dream from an early age, if not (ask God for your purpose) and begin to walk in it-on track- you will discover that you have love, peace, joy and happiness on earth. And everything in life will begin to make since; It just feels right.

A blessing is an empowerment to get wealth, prosperity. When I came upon this enlightenment phenomenally, I realized that life was not unlike a chess match, you and your mind against the normal and natural vicissitudes of life. Things that are just going to happen in life to cause growth, and some things like colds, flat tires, headaches etc. will appear for no apparent reason that we can understand.

One day I was day dreaming, nothing unusual for me that's what I like to do when my mind is free and clear. Before I learned to meditate the idea came to me unexpectedly concerning my life's work. My wishes to be thought of as comparable in conception as to be standing on a river bank just watching the waves go by and suddenly an old decaying tree branch came floating down the stream because its tree-mother from which it came had died. Once the limb passes you by it is soon forgotten. But if you see a tree limb floating down the same stream that has fruit, apples or pears on it, with green leaves, it will present to you a dichotomy of two thoughts. Follow the tree limb to see where it will end up, or go back up stream to see where it fell from, the most treasure! I began to look carefully and scrutinize every opportunity that engaged my path because God has answered all of my prayers twice thus far in my life. I chose to become creative in my thoughts and find out where they would take me.

I was twenty two years old when I graduated from college in 1972. I was offered a teaching job near my hometown in a neighboring county, one of my classmates was working there and suggested that I take it, it was a good opportunity according to him. However I had bigger and greater ideas about my future, I was going to think new thoughts and not follow anyone's advice about my future. I had choices and those choices would be directed by me and God alone. I realized that I was not born to follow anyone anymore, I would have to blaze my own trails because my thoughts did not fit into the average daily humdrum lifestyles without any challenges or chances to take and gain the greater prize. Even though my dream had been sidetracked, I was determined to find another way to accomplish my dreams. I would follow my dream downstream to see just where it would take me.

Being healthy of both mind, spirit and body, I cast my net by spreading the word around that I was seeking the opportunity to go to Columbia, SC, the decision that I made in the eighth grade on the State fair trip. I would test my skills at entering the business market if possible.

One Sunday evening after church I was at home watching a Pro-basketball game when suddenly I heard a car horn blow in our front yard. It was an upper classman from my high school who was now living in Columbia, perfect! An (alternate name) H. Laddy. He said that he had heard that I was looking for a ride to Columbia and this was it. H. Laddy not only took me to Columbia, he gave me a room in his apartment until I was able to pay rent. He took me around to apply for a couple of jobs and in that process I saw the sign that read channel 19 news and I said pull in here. He said you sure? yes. I went in and applied and was offered a job in the weather room. They said that there would be a two week waiting period to start at the beginning of the month, it would also give them the opportunity to complete all of the police (sled check) before I could start to work and training. I was broke and wanted to pay my own way, buy my own food etc. so in the meantime I was offered a job as a youth counselor at the South Carolina department of youth services now called DJJ. At DJJ I would become the first male counselor at an all girl school, Willow Lane school for girls.

The department intergraded the school with its first seventeen boys with ages ranging from age 9 thru 16. I really enjoyed greatly having the opportunity to mentor the first male students at the school. They said that they were waiting for the right guy to apply and be the first male counselor and it just happened to be me. While at Morris College, working in the bookstore for two years I took advantage of the opportunities given to read and study the development of many different observations of behavior and behavior modifications which allowed me to advance rapidly and acquire promotions rather quickly. I was enjoying the work so much that I plum forgot about the job that I had as a weather reporter at the TV station, probably just as well though, I knew that there would be lots of bosses at a TV station so I didn't have to make that choice. I played lots of basketball and taught ping pong techniques. It was fun I really enjoyed the work.

While on the home front though the first few days after I arrived in Columbia I met and encountered one of the most competitive young athletes that I had ever ran into. I met a young man who lived just across the street from me who didn't have the opportunity to go to college and he was phenomenal. I played against guys from almost every State and competed well, however none of them impressed me any way near the talents this guy had. I called him (alternate name) Coby Deed! This would become as a new door that I had opened and was clueless as to run into such people with athletic talents to beat me so definitively. I didn't think that there was anyone under six foot five that even had a chance against me.

Coby was six foot three and weighed 260 pounds with no fat, he was agile and quick in all directions, a pure shooter as well. We tied usually at two games each but he always managed to beat me three out of five games, he was tough under the basket and that's where he played me- one on one. After he beat me several days in a row I decided to see what else he could play. "Ping Pong" was a sport that I was excellent in I thought, I had speed, English and a back hand smash that was indefensible, unstoppable because of the English. Well he beat me three out five games in that too, but worse! We battled against each other in all sports and became the best of friends. When we played tennis though it made the word vindication sound sweet to me. The one sport that he couldn't hang with me in.

Celia and I became very close; she came to Columbia by bus to visit often. In November of 1972 I went down to Jim Moore Cadillac and Olds. car dealers on main St. I had been passing by often while riding with H. Laddy in his big beautiful Bonneville Pontiac, looking for the car that I wanted. One Sunday afternoon we stopped by to talk to a salesman and I just told the guy that I wanted to buy a 1972 cutlass Supreme, That's the car I thought had a prettier body style than a 1957 Chevy and the 1967 GTO Pontiac, call me when you get it. I told him emphatically that I was not interested in looking at anything else. In January 1973 just two months later the salesman called me one Sunday afternoon and told me that he had my car! My first car was a canary yellow, with a black convertible top and black leather bucket seats. It was the absolute prettiest car that I had ever seen. It had an eight track tape deck coupled with a cassette player as well. The first tape that I bought to play was "I paid the cost to be the boss" by James Brown, I drove down to Morris to show Celia my new car and guest what? What ED? She asked me to let her drive my brand new Cutlass Supreme down town, herself and some other girls. Didn't ask me to drive her, she wanted to drive on her own without me! I reluctantly gave her the keys before I knew it. Just like I patted her on her bottom before I knew it. I went inside the boys' dorm to talk to some of the guys who were at school when I left, the same two that I used to buy chicka-dee chicken for which tasted just like KFC'S chicken. I used to gamble and buy chicken and burgers to feed the guys from Rains who went to Morris. Well, while I was talking and laughing, kind of bragging you know, it darned on me that this girl Celia simply has too much nerve. Asking me to drive my brand new car which I only had it two days. And how come she didn't ask me to go? I don't believe that I'll be coming back over here if that's the way she's going to act, so I thought. I just couldn't get over this girl like the others. We continued dating and three days before Celia's graduation I asked her to marry me, but I wasn't thinking about right away, a couple, three years down the road perhaps. She boldly told me that she would, but I'm not waiting a long time at all on you to get married she said, or for me to make up my mind on a date. So we mutually agreed to wait at least one year. I knew nothing about rings so I took her down town to Kings Jewelers, staying with the Kings. I told her to pick out the ring that she wanted and she picked out a ring with a kind-a small diamond, I was glad because I had no idea that rings cost so much. Celia moved the date up twice and even though I was curious about how she was getting me to do all of these things that she wanted me to do, without me even questioning her once, I was keeping my eyes wide open and still it seemed that she was getting her way much too easily. I couldn't explain it.

While we were in the Jeweler's store and she was getting sized up, as usual I started to day dream about the first time that I saw her from the steps. She had the most perfectly shaped legs that I had seen in a long time. And the first time that I went to her dorm to formally introduce myself and to call on her for a date, she told me boldly as usual, I know who you are ED Graves, you are the best dressed guy on the campus and your home girls said that you were the same way in high school. And secondly, you are the great basketball player that everyone keeps asking you to join our basketball team so that we could win more games but you keep saying no!

Suddenly it occurred to me that Jesus had answered my prayers without me realizing it at all. I was twenty four years old; I had my Cutlass supreme, I was marrying the woman that I'd ask for by the time that I was twenty five and I had the job that I loved, with my first office. I was living in Columbia, the place that I had selected to make my home back in the eighth grade when I was only thirteen years old. It wouldn't be long before I purchased my very first home and had the two children that I ask God for, but five years apart rather than four which was fine with me.

THE HOLY SPIRIT RECEIVED

At the age of twenty three one Friday evening I felt very thankful that God had given me everything that I had asked him for. I was driving "Old Yella" the name that I had given my car. I was on a back road going to Mullins to pick up my oldest daughter's mother Pat, to go out on a date. I had decided and given it great thought over the years, it was time for me to give honor to Jesus by asking him to come into my heart and to be my personal savior. I was ready to change some things now that I was getting married and having a family, but not all things.

At that precise moment without hesitation, the Holy Spirit came and encompassed me and my entire body, from my head to my feet while driving along on the highway! I felt the mighty but calm and enormous power of the Almighty God, take over my body and spirit all at once! It was as if I had gently moved out of my body to be with the Lord.

When the experience was over it was as if I was slowly moving back into my body from outside of the car, I could see every small rock used to make the mixture that covered the road (highway) very clearly, even though the car was moving along, the headlights seemed to magnify my vision, as if I was looking through a magnifying glass. I went on and told my date that we wouldn't be going out that night, but after my spirit re-entered my body I found myself talking to the Lord but I couldn't recall what I was saying.

When I left Pat's house that night I went directly home to tell Mom, and to get some advice. Now understand me clearly, I did not give up all of my old ways immediately, didn't intend to, however I prayed constantly for guidance. I waited about two weeks before I asked God for my assignment, I was seeking guidance from spiritual leaders whom I thought should have known what to tell me to do. I was afraid that God was going to tell me to become a preacher but when I asked him finally, he told me to beware of women and alcohol, all of my answers would come in my later years.

On May 11, 1974 Celia and I were married in her home Church in Greenville South Carolina. I was twenty five years old just as I asked. Today I have two beautiful and loving daughters five years apart and we've been married for thirty one wonderful years. My third year at the SC. Department of DJJ I was promoted to assistant principal of the school with my own office! Within nine years after I prayed my prayer of petitions In college God had given unto me the wisdom to get all of the things that I had asked him for. I felt happy and complete, it would be years before my desires changed from being satisfied with being the assistant principal of a school, I really couldn't see myself doing anything else that would bring me more gratification than my current state of mind.

CHAPTER ELEVEN

Life as a Businessman

"Ralph Waldo Emerson" told us in one of his writings not to be a slave to your own past, plunge into the sublime seas, dive deep, and swim far with an advanced experience, that shall explain and overlook the old!

As the assistant principal I discovered that I had too many bosses. Each student and each parent, the Principal, the Superintendant, the school board and on up to the Governor of the State. After seven years I had had enough, I often found myself walking behind another man who was allowing my talents to flow through him without my approval. One day the Principal and I were talking and he told me that he too had decided to take the plunge into another profession, the insurance business.

Here I was working out of my own office as the assistant principal of a school with great benefits and good working conditions, however after a short while I was not happy, I became apprehensive after the principal resigned and went into the insurance business. The State personnel office hired someone from the outside and didn't even consider me for the position. The job description was pre-arraigned and drawn up to fit perfectly the guy that was chosen to replace him. I immediately started looking for an insurance company that had presence of mind, and a big name to carry behind me. I was being forced to make a decision to take the "chance to swim upstream"!

I saw an ad in the Sunday paper by Mutual of Omaha; This company owned the wild kingdom TV show. That was it, I looked no further, this one seemed and felt right!

In January of 1979 after seven years with the school system which gave me both safety and security, retirement benefits and the like, to go into the insurance business to work for commission only. The time had come for me to trust God and my own abilities. Leaving the school system was a giant step for me, my wife had all of the confidence in the world in me and had been telling me all along that I should open my own Insurance agency. Now the proper thing for me to do under the old thought processes and those in authority over me would strongly suggest that I consider the security of my wife and children and stay put, forever. The suggestion would have been seriously recommended for me to always get a good education, a good job with good benefits and stay with it until retirement and then take it easy.

My confidence has always been my best asset and now that I had recaptured it I wasn't going to let anything or anyone influence my thinking. My belief in authority had been destroyed long ago, many times so allowing someone else to dictate my success or failure was out. I had embarked upon a new freedom that I had never thought possible. In the Insurance business I was truly free in America with no strings. I and my family ate by the sales skills that I learned and developed in the training schools that the company offered. I wasn't punching any clocks or signing in with anyone, I was my own boss. I found freedoms and opportunities that I never dreamed of as a child. The hiring practices were such that only one out of every fifty people interviewed were hired. And then only the ones who scored the highest on their perspective achievement test made it past the interview. My scores were said to have been off the chart in all areas for success In both sales and management. On January 20, 1979 I boarded my first airplane to Miami Florida to attend the company's health insurance school.

When I arrived in Miami there was a long black Limousine waiting to take me to my hotel. I was taught sales techniques and product knowledge for one week. That Friday after classes we were all served prime rib steak with all of the deliquesces, my first even though I grew up on a large farm with several cattle.

After lunch the limo took me back to the hotel, The Four Ambassadors, four tall buildings aligned in semi-circular standings. When we arrived back I was amazed, "the Pittsburg Steelers and the Dallas Cowboys" were the featured attraction living in the same hotel occupying the first four floors in each building. It was "Super Bowl week" and they were getting up at four o'clock each morning, and going to practice without any interruptions from annoying fans. Mean Joe Green and all and I didn't get to see any of them. Folks like us would have been bugging those guys for autographs you know.

I flew first class on both flights going and coming, drinking Cutty sark and Ginger, I enjoyed it immensely! The Mutual of Omaha office in Columbia was comprised of thirty two white men and one white woman from Augusta GA. There was one black token salesman who studded in his speech and very shy. He was fired shortly after I came aboard, yeah you guessed it, I was supposed to become his replacement so they thought.

My very first week I earned over eleven hundred dollars in just four days. It was January still and very cold. I went to the bank to cash my check from the bank that my check was drawn from, right in the same office park on Forest Dr. The cashier looked at the check and looked back at me with a face full of curious looks of expression, I was dressed in a nice tie and blue suit, it didn't matter any, she called my division office and asked to speak to the manager. The manager answered the phone and as soon as he found out the purpose of the call was to inquire of him if I had somehow forged or stolen the check? He began to scream at the top of his voice, "WHAT DO YOU MEAN, DID HE STEAL THE CHECK", he went on to tell her that I was an excellent and powerful salesman. One of the best that I've ever had, needless to say that I was really proud to be free and black in America that day, the manager yelled so loudly on the phone that everyone in the bank heard it. Although the manager was from Mobile Alabama I found out later, actually just how he really felt about black people, I was the only black person in the bank that Tuesday along with a few older white ladies. It was explained to me by my unit manager later that the reasoning for our payday being scheduled to take place on Tuesdays was to always allow Agents to feel special and never have to wait in line for anything.

The cashier was inquiring as to how did I come by that much money on a Tuesday, the first week in February! That cashier got chewed out on the phone by my Division manager whose main objective is to see that the sales team earn substantial money for themselves, for the company, and earn money for him. I had just earned several thousands of dollars for the company and all involved for the next several decades. For the next several weeks I earned thousands of dollars per week, and it was during the heart of Winter. It changed my thinking completely. I had taken a chance and stepped through a new door of opportunity that I'd been dreaming of since I was four years old. After I was in the business for a couple of months I was cashing paychecks for three and four thousand dollars per week. It gave me a feeling of freedom that I had never known before. That cashier had in effect turned her back to me and called my office to inquire if I had stolen my own paycheck and I heard the manager threaten to move the company's funds from that bank, which was millions of dollars. He was yelling and cursing the cashier so loud and long until when she turned back to face me with a blood red face and watery looking eyes, the manager bluntly asked the cashier to give me the phone and she had to stand there while he gave me an apologetic assurance that it would never happen again.

All eyes in the bank were on her and she got called into her manager's office as I was leaving the bank!

When I went back to my office the manager apologized again and assured me that when those kinds of things happen to let him know because I had become a huge and positive player in the company's scheme of things. My production level had sat new standards for not only his office but the Home office as well. My production level of production In writing business had caused the white agents to improve their production levels all over the Country. They didn't want to be out sold by a black salesman such as myself. He said that the other Agents had begun to even dress better since I started to work there with my knowledge of color coordination in suits and ties. The division office manager and I had a good working relationship but my unit manager and I got along even better. He taught me many things about business and life in the business world as well. He was from Pittsburg and the kind of manager who rewarded agents for doing well, the way things in life are supposed to be, praised for doing good, and not sat up to fail!

Our office was in the tall five stories, Gold glass building on Forest Dr. on the fifth floor. We sat and talked many days about all sorts of things.

He blew me away when he told me that many white business owners get richer simply because of the fact that poor blacks always pay their bills late which forces them to have to pay late fees for rent, car loans, credit cards etc. The grocery store even change their prices on Wednesdays because black people get paid on Thursdays and Fridays and you'll only find black people in the stares on Thursday, Friday Saturday and mostly on Sundays. The shopping malls promote their sales on Monday and Tuesdays for white people because black people are usually broke on Mondays.

After my third year in the business I was always in the top second or third sales spot, never number one except in business group insurance. I was the top sales producer in group sales from my third year until I left in my tenth year. In 1982 I purchased my first home in Highland Park, a beautiful white ash colored brick home. In that very same year I found myself leaving the office one Friday afternoon, while walking to my car I looked back towards the building and the sun was peeking slightly over the of the building from the West. The sun light was glaring on the gold glass and sparkling beautifully, when suddenly, my mind reflected back and re-visited the photo of the young black man on the front page of the Ebony magazine that was given to me by my sister.

At that very moment as I opened my car door I realized that I had become that young man. I was dressed in a nice suit and tie, shoes shined and I had around two thousand dollars in my money clip. In those days one thousand dollar bills were easy to get from the bank, and I had two with some other denominations of bills. All of my dreams had come true just as I had imagined that it would with God's help. To include my two daughters, my home and cars, my own office and the ability to make millions. A loving wife, and I was only working two or three days per week, three or four hours per day, it seemed as if it didn't need to get any better than that, I loved what I was doing as far as work goes and didn't want to ever do anything else, I didn't even want the manager's job that they kept offering to me.

In the days to come, gently but persistently my wife told me that she and some of her friends at the school where she worked felt that I should leave Mutual of Omaha and open my own insurance agency. I had been in the State newspaper several times and the mutterings magazine often. I Had been asked to appear in the Wild Kingdom show's commercial. The more my wife asked me to quit my job the more I thought about how she talked me into letting her drive my new Cutlass Supreme. She left me standing there watching the tail lights of my new beautiful and shiny car drive out of the gates of the campus. I said to myself, daah gal must be crazy! Got my new car and gone! Gaaait day! I must be crazy for giving it to heh. I didn't even ask to see her driving license, how dumb can you get Arvanie! Wah in de world am I standing here for and my car is gone.

At the time I thought that it was the silliest thing that I had ever heard, asking me to quit the job that I'd wanted all of my life, she didn't know squat about business, so I would live to regret not taking the advice of the basic intuitive intrinsic nature of the woman that I loved.

Typically in the eighties everything seemed to flourish in my world, the world of business. My manager had complete confidence in me and my abilities, he referred to me as his go to guy, Just like Jim Brown's coach said about him. When the office needed extra production in order to win a contest National competition, my manager took me out to the steak and ale to discuss strategy. Those contest were based on a point system and I won several trips to various places around the country and abroad. Meanwhile from a religious standpoint my relationship with Jesus Christ was seriously suffering. Soon after I received the Holy Spirit in my car I joined a local Baptist Church.

The church that I joined was St. John Baptist church and it was perfect for me at the time, due the promise that I made to myself the day that I graduated from high school. I promised myself that I would never go to another Holiness church as long as I lived because of the way that they refused to allow me to join and accept Christ as my personal savior. They wanted me to fake the Holy Ghost and show the quickening of the spirit openly before the Church at that moment.

I was baptized along with four other children one Sunday evening and given the right hand of fellowship by the pastor and the congregation, I felt the congenially of the saints of the church immediately. This Church had six different choirs and I didn't have to teach because there were several qualified teachers there. For some reason though I couldn't seem to pay all of my tithes as I should have, no matter how much money that I made. I was selfish and there's no other way to put it. My money always seemed to find other places to go on its own, but God was about to teach me a valuable lesson concerning his money.

One Sunday morning in the early nineties I heard the calm small voice that I was so familiar with say to me, ED I don't need your gifts and talents here in this Church, you must go back to the Church of your youth and build from there. Well, that Church was well over one hundred miles away, so I knew that there had to be a Holiness Church closer that I was supposed to find somehow.

Meanwhile my tax situation had come to a head at work with the IRS, It had taken a serious nose dive. In one year I owed the IRS over twenty seven thousand dollars and it quickly rose to forty thousand with the interest and penalties applied and steadily rising. I went down and made an agreement with the IRS to pay five hundred dollars per month on those taxes, and I was still expected to pay my estimated taxes as well. I was living in my second home which was much larger than my first one. At Mutual there was an organization called Presidents club that only the best and most productive Agents could attain and for eight out ten years that I was at Mutual of Omaha, I was a regular of that club. Only the first two years I wasn't able to make it because I was traveling to and fro the training schools that I attended in Omaha and Miami Florida.

Unfortunately I was late by only one day with my payment to the IRS and they came to my home, confiscated two of my vehicles and forced the sale of my home to get their money. I had to move my family into a hotel for a while and in as much as I tried to maintain, I was forced to resign from Mutual of Omaha, the company that I loved. The IRS was garnishing one hundred percent of my wages they had no pity, I went to my Division Manager because my unit manager had been transferred to another State office. I talked my situation over with him and applied for my deferred compensation which was over four hundred thousand dollars, however my portion was only two hundred and thirty seven thousand. It would be enough to open my own agency office at last, so I thought;

Would you believe that this Division manager devised a method of paying off my IRS debt for me, and supposedly cut a check to me for the balance, so he told me. Instead he devised his own method of drafting funds from my deferred compensation account fund, and sending out new hired agents and some old Agents to my policy holders, having them sign a new agent form because I was to have retired suddenly, giving those policy holders a since of urgency to switch agents. Now get this clearly, the manager charged me back the commissions that I earned seven and eight years back, all commissions that I had been paid to me over the past ten years and didn't pay the IRS a single dime.

There was no applied rule to charge an agent back commissions unless the policy was dropped or lapsed within the first six months to one year in some cases. In all actuality, he was robbing me blind and there was absolutely nothing that I could do about it. I thought that it was impossible for an employer to touch an employee's deferred compensation. I found out different, I hired an Attorney; There was an occasion when the Presidents club producers were invited to a company paid vacation in Los Angeles California, and my wife accompanied me on the trip. Surprisingly I met the only other black Agent from South Carolina, Florence that is, the gentleman was a preacher who pastured his own church in Bishopville SC. I believe that it happened in Devine order that I heard the Holy Spirit say to me, you must go back to the church of your youth and build from there. Build what I thought? Well he invited me and I begun to attend regularly, before long I joined his church, a Pentecostal Church.

In California Celia and I visited Universal studios, the place that the company leased for the entire week for us. We visited the J.Paul Getty museum, we saw Howard Hughes famous plane, the Spruce Goose, and we had dinner by candle light on the Queen Mary ship, the trip was wonderful. They actually put me on the movie screen. We saw the musical play "cats" before it ever received its first review. The ten years that I spent at Mutual of Omaha were the happiest of my adult life, anything that my family or I wanted, I made it happen, but now it was all about to change.

CHAPTER TWELVE

"Downward Spiral"

Many times I contacted the home office by letter because I wasn't allowed to talk directly to the higher ups, now that I had initiated litigation with my Attorney against the company. The only thing that the personal office department would do at that time was to just make a copy of my letter for the office records, and mail a copy back to my former division office manager. The Home office supported anything that he told them completely, I was on my own, the division manager managed to develop personal communications with my white Lawyer to his benefit also. Here I was again, at the mercy of someone in authority over me as usual, what can I say, quit-give up, not a chance; God was expanding my territory through human betrayal!

There would be people that God placed into my life that I was supposed to follow for a while and move on, but I was exactly where I always wanted to be. Lessons most times are painful just before the new horizons appear to propel you into the next stage of your destiny, a "chess match".

I vowed to continue to dive deep, and take the necessary chances to overcome any obstacle that showed up in my life, fear or quitting was not an option for me at this point.

In 1990 I began to drink more heavily and not just to reward myself for doing well in business as I had in the past. I was in a state of deep depression, my family of four were living in a one room hotel sweet, my daughters were at the ages of eight and thirteen and I had to transport them to two different schools without letting the schools know that we had moved out of the appropriate districts. I also had to transport my wife to the school where she taught so there wasn't enough time in my day to effectively earn a living. I asked my brother who was living in Columbia if he could store my furniture in his garage for a short while, just for a short while for me to regain my footing but he denied me the favor. I had to place all of our worldly goods in a storage garage and lost everything when I couldn't pay the third months storage rent. We even lost our wedding pictures, everything.

The IRS closed all of my bank accounts, business checking account, and personal checking and saving accounts and seized everything. I had written checks to cover my living expenses and all of the checks bounced, and kept on dribbling! I went to DSS for help and they told us that my wife would have to quit her teaching job, while I found a way to dispose of the balance of my deferred compensation account that was being savagely stolen by my former division office manager, but I couldn't touch it. I was locked from the top and the bottom! Moreover the manager was listing my compensation with the home office as an undetermined amount of debt that I owed him, while he charged me back through my account until it was all gone! I was completely alone, there was no friend or family member that I could turn to, except God;

In June, the fourteenth day, my oldest daughter's birthday in 1990 she was fourteen, the two sevens showed up, my numbers for good and the bad, some thing significant always happened in my life. I drove down to my mail box to pick up the monetary gifts that my in-laws always gave. By the way my mother and father in law always stood by us. The police had been looking for me, I had racked up four DUI'S all about four months apart, this stop would be my fifth, and as luck would have it, I wasn't drinking so it became a driving under suspension. I had been writing bad checks to feed my family and pay my hotel bill on a closed account.

So, I got locked up on my daughter's fourteenth birthday and had no means to make bail anymore. The night before I was to go before the Judge I was laying on a cot with absolutely nothing in terms of earthly possessions, inside or outside of the jail. I was looking in the face of hopelessness; it was a long way for me to fall from where I was just a year ago. The only earthly possession that I had was my ability to think! I remembered a writing where King Solomon said" when you are dead, you cannot even think a good thought.......This is where some people commit suicide, I had fallen over seven times already and didn't see the end of my life in sight. Down on the grown is no place for a "KING". I said Jesus, you said that you would always be with me, well we're going to prison now, I'm already in jail. I began to think new thoughts on that cot, thoughts of the invisible world of spirit where Jesus is. I was facing the possibility of three years for each of my four DUI'S, Twelve years, and I didn't know how many for the bad checks, someone said up to three years. They had let me keep my wedding band and my Masonic ring. I began to re-live the events of my life in groups of seven. Seven lean years and seven bountiful years.

I was trying to figure "Why"? How could this happen to me, even though I wasn't living as Jesus wished. I could feel his presence, he was with me now and I had no trepidation what so ever in my heart, no fear. I begun by apologizing to Jesus for my reckless behavior and disobedience. I was hesitant because I was ashamed, not only had I let my family down but Jesus as well. I began to talk to Jesus in that room as if he was sitting on the bunk right beside me, actually he was because I could feel his powerful presence.

"Jesus"

Now that you have my undivided attention such that I have no other recourse but to listen to you and only you before I give you my petition. I wish to apologize and to say that I'm sorry for being so negligent with all of the gifts that you have given me. There is nothing that can make me feel any worst than I feel at this moment. You have always been with me and I have no doubt that you are here with me right now. What should I say to the Judge in the morning? Softly and gently the words of Deuteronomy, chapter eight and eleven appeared in my mind (Beware that thou forget not the Lord thy God,---also prepare not what thou should say, for I knew that he would give me the words at the prescribed moment

When they called me to go to court the next morning for sentencing, some men in the line told me that I could get up to fifteen years for my charges, but it didn't register with me. I had also spoken to a public defender whose advice to me was to not say anything in court, she would do all of the talking. That didn't register either, it was my first time in jail and I wasn't listening to anyone but Jesus!

The municipal court house on North Main St. was packed and the court room was huge. There was a white woman Judge sitting on the bench that day and people were being sent to prison left and right. There was a young man whom had been sitting beside me in the holding cell was charged with first degree murder. I asked him what had happened and he said to my surprise, the other guy made me kill him, I was shocked. All of the guys locked up seemed to know each other, I knew no one and I was forty years old. I was from a different background entirely, moreover it was highly unusual that someone like myself, a businessman with a college degree would be in such a predicament as this. Most of the other men that I had met in here were on drugs or alcohol, unemployed with an impoverished background. they were mostly repeat offenders with long arrest records. However my condition appeared from the surface not that unusual. The Judge read my charges and my public defender said, we plead guilty your Honor, and that was it? That's all I said? No mitigating circumstances or otherwise. Then the Judge looked at me and said is there anything that you wish to say sir before I pass sentencing? Well I make my living talking, there's no way that I'm going to stand here and leave my life in the hands of this incompetent public defender. I acted as if she wasn't even there. It was as if I had seen the jawbone of the ass that Samson saw! I spoke calmly, clearly and without fear of the consequences that I faced. I knew that King Solomon discovered early on in his reign the distinctive and intuitive nature of a woman, and so did I. I knew that she would hear and understand my dilemma!

I explained to the Judge that my wife and two young daughters were living in a hotel room not far from here. The police had seized three automobiles from me and the IRS had seized my home. I explained my inability to get my deferred compensation and the whole saga of it being seized as we spoke here today. The only way that I could keep my family together was to write the bouncing checks, no one would give us any help. I went on to tell her that we as a family had enjoyed a wonderful and successful life and career, myself as an insurance broker and my wife as an elementary school teacher. I was interrupted rudely by a disgruntle probation officer who had come to my home to tell me that a Judge had ordered me to pay forty five dollars per week in fees and that he didn't care in the lease that all of my earnings were being garnished by the IRS. I had taken hold of the white probation officer's collar and the seat of his pants, and thrown him out on my driveway. Needless to say that he was highly upset, and only interested in seeing me go to Prison for a long time.

The Judge told him right then and there that if he spoke out of term again she would hold him in contempt of Court. Mr. Graves, please continue, before I could speak the probation officer said, but Judge he owes check fees; The Judge said fifty dollars fine and instructed the police to place him under arrest for five days. The Judge then asked me? Mr. Graves, what level of education do you have? I graduated from college your Honor. She said that it was unusual that she had a college graduate in her courtroom. She told the Court that she hoped that everyone was listening and paying very close attention to the eloquence and definitive verbal command of displaying my circumstances before the court. She said that she was not used to having anyone speak with such correct English. The Judge started scribbling or writing notes or whatever, and then she held her head up and said, Mr. Graves, I certainly can understand your dilemma, especially involving the IRS and the garnishment of your total wages.

Mr. Graves I'm going to give you one year for driving under suspension and I'm throwing out all of your DUI'S. I'm going to further – disregard all of the bad checks, I'm sending you to Walden correctional on Broad River road for one year to get your finances in order; Once again the probation officer stood up and said, but your Honor, he has several bad checks that have bounced around town. The Judge said $100.00 fine and ten days in jail for contempt! She told the court, this young man has the bad checks because the IRS garnished all of his wages totally, dismissed! As I was being escorted out of the courtroom by two police officers from Florence, near my home, one of them was so astonished until he told me that the Judge was sending me to a work release camp and the only time that I would have to do was six months. He said that if he ever needed a Lawyer he was going to come and see me, no Lawyer in the State could have done any better than you did in here today.

The Judge would be sending me to a work release camp where I would be released every day to work in my own business for six months. I became a hero in the courtroom that day and little did I know that it would surely follow me into prison as well, and for good measure.

When I arrived at Walden Correctional everyone knew my name including the Warden and all of the officers, it seems that some of the guys from Walden were in court with me that day. That's how quickly news travels in prison, everyone wanted me to look over their warrants to see what advice I could give on their behalf. God was showing me favor just like he did Joseph in the bible when his brother sold him into slavery and he ended up in prison.

The prison was just like the courtroom was, 98% black and over half of them came to me for advice, over eleven hundred men was in Walden. I had never been in prison, unlike spending one night in the county jail now and again for drinking and driving. I would find out if it were true what I saw on TV about prison life and the jokes told in general, I was prepared to fight and I was looking forward to it before I got too old. I was in prison for no other reason than to have all of my deferred compensation stolen and being broke! How do you like that, being taken advantage of had caused me to become a criminal.

Waldon was a non-violent prison camp and nothing like I thought that it would be. It was like living in a college dorm except we didn't have doors or walls all the way up to the ceiling, they only walls were about four feet high, we could stand up and look over the entire dorm. A wide open bay area, no one was locked up in a cell at Walden, men could walk to and fro as they pleased. No bars or doors slamming shut, and every morning at six o'clock Sharpe everyone was allowed to walk out of the dorm for breakfast and work, those that wanted to work and get paid.

My very first night I had a dream as did Joseph, Jacob's son in the Bible. I was shown favor because I had an education and ninety percent of the men (inmates) were high school dropouts or thrown outs. They couldn't read or write legibly. I had worked at DJJ and I knew most of the Judges in the State and coupled with the fact that I was of the Masonic order I was perceived as having great power. I was asked to write several Judges on behalf of inmates who had pending charges in order to get them ran concurrent with the time that they were already serving, to get an early release date. I taught GED courses and my roommate just happened to be very good cook in the dining hall. Every night he brought me steaks smothered in onions and gravy, fried chicken and almost any food that you could get on the outside. I gained forty pounds in the six months and gave up drinking even though it was brought in every day. I studied my Bible and thought over my past life, I remembered that I had writing skills and a love for it, it was relaxing.

When I was released in March of 1991 I had no driving license for the next nine years and no car. I had to have a driver's license to do what I did for a living, I was a professional salesman and loved it. I asked my Brother Billy to take me to Baltimore, I got a Maryland driver's license the next day and started working for the Baltimore Sun newspaper selling newspaper subscriptions as a telemarketer. Soon I was working part-time at the MBNA America bank selling credit cards over the phone all over the US. The following year I went to work at Lamtum light bulb company selling light bulbs and having them shipped all over the Country as well. Everywhere I went I sat trail blazing sales records and when the word got around of my sales ability and telephone techniques', my phone was ringing off the hook daily, everyone wanted to offer me a job.

NEW CHALLENGES IN NEW CITY

In 1970 I spent a year in Baltimore MD. During a time when the economy was flourishing and everyone who wanted to work was working, this was not the case this time. As soon as I earned enough money to buy a car I went back into the Insurance business with Metropolitan life and health as a sales manager, however I continued to experiment with the telemarketing business that I had established. The Holy Spirit was leading me into a new direction now that I was in this new environment. My intentions were to leave as soon as I could get a car but I still had my license suspended in South Carolina, and interesting sales companies were constantly calling and spiking my interest for telephone sales jobs.

Each new sales job that I went on I sat new and blazing sales records, time after time and every place that I went. Before I knew it four years had passed and I wasn't seeing nearly enough of my family but I finally found out what was keeping me in Baltimore. I took the challenge of fundraising by phone and I really liked raising money for good causes, I found out that many citizens arbitrarily make commitments to donate thousands of dollars each year to various charities. Some were donating their tithes to worthy causes over the phone. I took a job with an outfit who ha d a contract to raise money for the Maryland Special Olympics and the Multiple sclerosis foundation part-time. I was raising upwards of three thousand dollars in four hours over the phone, whereas the top producer in the office was only raising $400.00 in eight hours tops. That's just how much more I was raising over veteran producers everywhere that I went. It was like that at Mutual of Omaha also. The owners of the company were three young Italian Americans all under thirty years of age and here I was at forty one years old, making these guys rich.

The owners made me a fantastic offer to manage a new location of theirs but I knew what God was trying to show me just what he wanted me to do now. Being taken back to the memory of being in prison I remembered a special dream that I had. The Holy Spirit showed me many things pertaining to my failures in life. I was actually living my dream before the downward spiral downfall, living a life of luxury with all of my needs being met. I was on my way to earning millions through a payroll deduction through an employee plan that I sat up with the State and Federal employees to sell life and disability insurance deducted automatically through their paychecks.

In my dream I was flying in an L-10-11 airplane, the same one that I always used on all business and personal trips. As the plane begun to elevate to three, four and then six thousand feet above sea level, I saw cars as I looked down that looked like tiny ants moving in different directions. Trees that looked like shrubbery, and the ground looked like a map on the page of a book. When the plane moved above the clouds I saw the endlessness and boundlessness of the universe, I heard a familiar voice speak to me saying, look to the east corner! I saw in my spirit beautiful and shiny glittering like diamonds, rubies and sparkling like pearls! I saw the most beautiful multicolored flowers with multi-fragranced odors I had ever smelled. I heard the most beautiful sounding chorus with blends of coloraturas, base and baritone voices that I had ever dreamed of. I said to myself, Mahailia Jackson is still waiting in line to get on this choir. And church folk everywhere are talking about singing and shouting around Jesus all day every day, I think not. The voice said to me, "you have become complacent and satisfied with your life the way that it is" You have no desire to go on to your chosen destiny. You've refused to continue growing and learning as well as teaching. You will find your answer in Baltimore, and then he showed me a new building with strange letterings and my name at the bottom.

A strong since of realization embraced my mind, not only had I been making these companies richer that I worked for in the past, now I knew that I could build a business for myself without too much of an original start up investment. I had the same dream about once per month, using my skills to make someone else richer.

Finally I quit all of those jobs that I was working on at my leisure and left Baltimore and went back to my family in Columbia. I immediately went to work for a non-profit company as a fundraiser in 1995. As always I was the leader in the department and one day while sitting at my desk during my break, all of a sudden I felt an overwhelming restless feeling as if I wasn't doing anything worthwhile with my skills. I was bored and contemplating quitting, this job was a temporary stop for me anyway. I started to think about the name of my new company, a non-profit business that I was going to start. I realized why I was moving from job to job in Baltimore and I knew that God was showing me the different avenues that I could take as an entrepreneur.

I started thinking of names for my business, I knew that I was going to start a job training business for youth to curb the involvement in "gangs and drugs". I came up with a slogan, athenaeum to help get kids back on track.

ON TTRACC was born, Technical Training Resolves Anticipated Community Crime! In 1997 after spending several months in the Library I received my 501-c-3 from the Federal Government. I continued on researching and developing fundraising and grant writing skills on my own.

When it came down to establishing the building process of opening a Bible Business College there was no one that I could turn to for advice. I went to the place that I knew what King Solomon meant when he said a wise man is not one who memorizes dates and events, scriptures that other wise men wrote, instead, a wise man knows where to go for answers when you have a problem that no one seems to be able to help you. I went to the library as usual and quickly found out that there's no Bible Business colleges in existence, in the world, ON TTRACC would become the first.

The new chess match began, there would have to be a planning period to establish a registrar's office, a restaurant or cafeteria, Business office to operate centrally. The thought arose with this thinking, The Holy Spirit made it crystal clear that I was in my later years which meant that the gifted woman at Coney Island in New York, the messenger was right; It was time that I except my calling into the Ministry that I was avoiding for so long.

A few years back at a Pentecostal Church in Cayce SC.- West Columbia, shortly after I transferred from the Church in Bishopville, The Bishop appointed me as the Sunday School teacher after a female assistant Pastor made a grave mistake, a misrepresentation of the scripture while she was teaching one Sunday morning. I politely corrected her, now surely I don't have to spell out the type of relationship that she and I had afterwards. Teaching Sunday school every Sunday was preparing me for my ministry, and I realized that God was moving the chess pieces. That awareness grew as time passed and I enjoyed the experience.

At the Church in Cayce there was a small congregation with only three males so I volunteered to except the responsibilities of maintenance man for the Church. One Saturday after I finished cutting the Church grass for free, I went inside to cool off and as I sat down just relaxing, thinking, the thought came to me as I was daydreaming as usual, this is a good time to practice my trial sermon, Jesus would be my only audience. I brushed myself off and went into the pulpit, opened the Bible and took my text. I began to preach to the invisible world of spirit. The Bishop had already told me to talk with my Pastor, who was a female also from the Charleston area, and set up a date for me to preach my initial sermon, the Bishop and I were friends.

I told the pastor the following Sunday that the Bishop wanted me to set a date for me to preach my initial sermon as soon as possible. She said ok but I found out that working for God in Ministry was not going to be any different than it was when I was displaying my talents on my high school basketball team. The female pastor conveniently managed to put off my sermon month after month until one day The Bishop and I were having breakfast at our favorite restaurant and he asked me if I had completed my sermon yet, he was ready to give me an assignment. Two years had passed so I told Bishop that he would have to set the date for me to preach himself. The next Saturday Bishop sat up a council meeting at our church in Cayce and made the announcement that I would be preaching my trial sermon the following Sunday. I had a terrible cold but there's no way that I was going to pass up this opportunity to take the next step towards my destiny. The big day I was accompanied in the pulpit by my female pastor, the female assistant Pastor and the Bishop. The title of my message was "What is man that we should acknowledge him" When I finished the message the Bishop stood up to confirm and welcome me into the field of ministry and just like my uncle did in my home church when I tried to join the Church, the Bishop said to the Pastor, well, how did brother Graves do? She replied, well, I had to preach my trial sermon five times, he turned to the female assistant Pastor for a possible confirmation, not so, she said, he wasn't even preaching he was just teaching; It was my understanding that when God calls you to preach, who can deny or flunk you? I was blown away again! The Bishop looked at me and said sadly, well, brother Graves will be called brother Graves a while longer instead of REVERAND Graves; That following week the assistant Pastor forced the Pastor out of her job as pastor and she assumed the authority and roll as Pastor of the Church in Cayce.

The very next Sunday when the assistant Pastor took over as Pastor of the Church she printed out assignments for everyone in the Church except me. There were only twenty members in the Church and she arraigned for everyone to be present that day. She came down from the pulpit and commenced to calling out the names of each member, handed them a certificate of assignment, had all to take a seat on the opposite side of the Church and left brother ED Graves sitting on the right side of the Church alone. I politely stood up and said that I'm requesting a transfer immediately, I know exactly where this is going. The exact same thing was raising its ugly head again the same way that it was in high school.

"How Mercy".

I had decided long ago that I wouldn't allow anyone in authority over me ever again to stand in the way of my destiny ever again. There's absolutely no way that I'm going back to see Jesus through the grave and tell him that I couldn't do what he told me to do because some woman preacher from the North wouldn't let me do what I was supposed to do.

When I was at Morris College I took the opportunity to get to know every preacher on campus. Not only was I immensely impressed with the practice sessions held in the dorms that they conducted, and how they interjected their text and capturing the subject which was ingrained in the message. Another thing, the preachers always had Kentucky fried chicken! I found myself sitting In the theology for ministers classes many times, listening to various preachers do their thing.

My older sister was married to a military minister and he is indeed someone that I'm very proud of. One Sunday he preached at my home Church in Rains and I was afraid that he was out of his league preaching behind the great and famous Rev. Mannie McCall. He began his message by charismatically strolling into his introductory description of God by saying, God is so good, God is so great, God is so BEAUTIFUL!!! I had invited some friends to hear him and they were impressed.

The assistant pastor now pastor even gave my maintenance job to someone, the job that I was doing for free. Now let's not forget that this was a Pentecostal Church just like the Church that I said that I would never set foot inside ever again. I was only in this Church because God expressed to me that I should go here to begin to build my ministry.

I arraigned a meeting with the Bishop and told him what had transpired and that I had requested a transfer. I went on to tell him that many other ministers under his authority would feel threatened just like those two female preachers at Cayce does because of my ability to discern the scriptures and more importantly because I was the founder of a Bible Business College. I felt that I would not be welcomed at those Churches either. However the Pastor in Bishopville was a good friend, I thought? He was the founder of his own Church and a successful businessman in the insurance business same as I was, I believed that he will surely welcome me, besides, he was the one who's responsible for getting me back into the Pentecostal church. Bishop said well it's settled then, go to Bishopville and preach your trial sermon there and be ready to come back when I call you. I was driving fifty miles one way to church on Sunday and Wednesdays.

That was January 2007, in July of 2007 I preached my trial sermon but before I was allowed to preach I was counseled thoroughly by the Pastor who I thought was my friend. First he tried to tell me what to preach, after that he tried to give me one of his old sermons to preach but I refused, I had to preach what God gave me to deliver.

The night that I preached my initial sermon my cousin from Mullins came, also my cousin from high school came, the General Elder and assistants. The title of my message was, "The night before Jesus Trial, a witness appeared in the bedroom of Pontius Urelious Pilot". The congregation roared the entire message and when I finished the Gen. Elder stood up and said this preacher is going right straight to the top. The Pastor who I thought was my friend leaned over to me and said, you want be preaching in here anymore anytime soon. From that day followed many degradations against me and persecutions from the pulpit, he thought that his church was desiring to follow me instead of him. I finally filed a grievance against him which resulted in me filing a police report and a civil lawsuit against him for stealing and embezzling money that I paid to the Church. I was persecuted more by him than anyone else until I fought back and won.

CONCLUSION

Favorably God has allowed me to attain my dreams from the age of four until now. I've suffered many trials and overcome numerous obstacles simply by keeping my faith in him. There were times when the father had to force me into my destiny, in order to move past comfort zones. I had to endure three brief trips to prison, at three to six month intervals each along the way before I was able to receive what God had promised me. Thankfully I only suffered mistomeaner charges, no felonies. The only reason that I ever went to prison was because my division office manager embezzled my deferred compensation money which methodically caused my IRS problem. However I've long since gotten past this matter but how do you get past being treated badly by a coach for doing good! There's no way to recapture the ages of 17, thru age 22, when one is discovering the capabilities of his own body. Mental abuse is a terrible thing, forgiveness is the only solution.

In Bishopville I was reminded of an athletic invention that I wasn't doing anything with. I have developed and applied for a patent for it which is now pending. I've never had a tennis lesson but just like I developed my basketball skills, I fell in love with the tennis games of Author Ash and Jimmy Connors by way of TV which allowed me to become the amateur tennis player of my division in 1976 as well as ping pong champion of the year. I've never taken a typing or computer literacy course in my life, I taught myself writing this book. I'm grateful for the gifts that God has given me.

Now seems to be a good place to make mention of my friend McGill of McGill's funeral home in Marion SC. The checker king!

Dean Bell and Joe Bethea, fella's whom I kept in supply of Chic-a-Dee chicken at Morris College, these men are certainly making God smile with the work that they are doing in the Church. Rev. A.C. Robinson, who is developing and building some great things for our community. My good friends Charles and Glenn D. Pee. My cousin Rev. Willie N.Pee who is the character LiL Bill Tee in this book and my cousins Leo, Maceo Carver, Patricia and Leon Philips. Maceo operates the Bible teaching Barber shop in Mullins, good friend Jacks Barber shop. My cousins Mildred Ann, Barbara Jean and especially Diane Edwards. Ruby and Essie Mae Curry, Bo Bell, Travis, My classmate and friend Victoria Belin, Sherman Belin, my friend who suffered the same fate by the coach in college. It is my honest opinion that Ed Graves, Dean Bell, Sherman Belin and my high school coach's son, given the exposure would have played in the NBA. My good friend Roosevelt Eddy, and entrepreneur, and Leon Godbolt.